Higher Education and the Market

The introduction of market forces into higher education is the most crucial issue facing universities and colleges today. As the role of universities in the knowledge society becomes ever more apparent, and as public funding reaches its limit, marketisation has become an issue of critical importance. Discussions about the ever-increasing cost of tuition, affordability, access, university rankings, information and the commercialization of academic research take place not just in North America, Western Europe and Australasia, but also in Eastern Europe, Asia and Latin America.

Higher Education and the Market provides a comprehensive account of this phenomenon, and looks at its likely impact on key dimensions of university activity:

- system structure
- funding and resources
- the curriculum
- participation and achievement
- research and scholarship
- interactions with third parties

Contributors propose how market forces, government intervention and academic self-regulation can be combined to harness the benefits of increased competition and efficiency without losing the public good. It is of particular interest to government and institutional leaders, policy makers, researchers and students studying higher education.

Roger Brown is Co-Director for the Centre of Higher Education Research Development (CHERD) at Liverpool Hope University.

Higher Education and the Market

Edited by Roger Brown

Routledge
Taylor & Francis Group

NEW YORK AND LONDON

First published 2011
by Routledge
270 Madison Avenue, New York, NY 10016

Simultaneously published in the UK
by Routledge
2 Park Square, Milton Park, Abingdon, Oxon OX14 4RN

Routledge is an imprint of the Taylor & Francis Group, an informa business

© 2011 Taylor & Francis

Typeset in Minion by
Swales & Willis Ltd, Exeter, Devon
Printed and bound in the United States of America on acid-free paper by
Walsworth Publishing Company, MO

Library of Congress Cataloging in Publication Data
Higher education and the market / edited by Roger Brown.
p. cm.
Includes bibliographical references and index.
1. Education, Higher—Economic aspects—Cross-cultural studies.
2. Education, Higher—Marketing—Cross-cultural studies. I. Brown, Roger, 1947–
LC67.6.H53 2010
338.4'3378—dc22
2009052424

ISBN 13: 978–0–415–99168–1 (hbk)
ISBN 13: 978–0–415–99169–8 (pbk)
ISBN 13: 978–0–203–84900–2 (ebk)

This book is dedicated to Jack and Betty Brown.

Table of Contents

List of Tables and Figures

Tables

Figures

Foreword

American higher education is a generally considered by most observers to be a tremendous success story. It has surpassed every other system in combining access with excellence. Following the passage of the Servicemen's Readjustment Act, more generally known as the G.I. Bill, after World War II, it has consistently educated a higher proportion of the population than any of its main rivals. At the same time, its leading institutions have dominated the international university rankings. The most recent *Times Higher Education* rankings show American universities holding 13 of the top 20 spots (*Times Higher Education, 2009*). Its excellence is also demonstrated by its continuing attractiveness to students and graduates from overseas. So it is hardly surprising that the American system has become the model for many other countries not only in respect of student education but also in academic research and in wider service and engagement.

One major reason for this success is the competition built into the system. The first colleges in colonial America were private institutions, generally affiliated with religious organizations but independent of the colonial governments. While some of these institutions received support from the government, they had their own boards and were free from political control. Beginning in the late eighteenth century, after the founding of the country, states began chartering public universities to complement the still-growing market for private higher education (Heller, 2002).

As this mixed public–private system grew, market entry was controlled but liberal. Competition on price accompanied competition on quality. All of this created a system remarkable for its diversity, responsiveness and innovation. These features were reinforced by the passage of the Higher Education Act of 1965, when federal support for higher education institutions was channelled through students rather than directly to the institutions themselves. This was accompanied in the ensuing decades by a huge inflow of philanthropic funds which remains unique in scale and importance.

But there is another side to the picture. The American system no longer looks so astonishing, as other countries have met or surpassed our enrolment rates (OECD, 2009). There is a crisis of affordability which threatens to set back the progress previously made on access. At the same time, completion rates have deteriorated, a natural consequence of expanding access to populations of students who are not as prepared academically for postsecondary study. Colleges and universities are struggling to produce enough graduates in areas vital for the nation's future competitiveness, such as science and technology. The very factors that have made the system so effective—a high degree of institutional autonomy, mixed ownership and funding, and intense competition—now seem to be holding it back.

In *Higher Education and the Market* Roger Brown and his colleagues show that some of these problems are not unique to America. To be sure, market competition can encourage universities and colleges to be more efficient, more innovative, and more responsive to students and research funders. But because of the difficulties of defining and measuring quality, such competition can easily deteriorate into positional competition, the academic "arms race" described by so many commentators. Stratification—both amongst institutions and amongst the populations they serve—replaces diversity. Quality stagnates as institutions invest in things that will attract students and funders rather than improve the quality of education provided. The net result is that society may be getting less value from the enormous resources it invests in higher education than it should. There is also a damaging loss of trust if universities become more like commercial enterprises aiming to maximise revenues rather than intellectual communities seeking to maximise knowledge.

Higher Education and the Market breaks new ground not just in describing and analysing this phenomenon but in putting forward wide-ranging but realistic solutions. The book argues that both public and private institutions need to be regulated if the full range of public benefits of higher education—such as a well-trained workforce, an educated citizenry, new knowledge and know-how—is to be maximised. Competition for students and research funders should continue but within broadly prescribed limits. The academic community should remain responsible for standards and quality but should be much more explicit about the ways in which these are protected. A regulator independent of both government and institutions should ensure that wherever a student studies she should receive a worthwhile return for her time and resources. Such regulation should also monitor the conduct of commercially funded research. Fresh efforts should be made to integrate the core academic activities of teaching and research so that each benefits the other.

A few years ago such a programme might have seemed unrealistic, even utopian. But with the recent failures in the financial markets still fresh in our minds (and pockets), it no longer seems so. *Higher Education and the Market* does not reject market competition, or private support for a nation's universities. But it does show why and how both need to be constrained within an appropriate policy framework if the full benefits—both public and private—of a healthy higher education system are to be fully realised. Although it draws on the experience of a number of major systems worldwide it has a particular resonance for America. It is therefore hoped that it will be studied carefully by everyone

xii · Donald Heller

who is concerned about the current direction of American higher education, and the implications that direction has for systems in other countries.

Dr Donald Heller
Professor of Higher Education
Head of the Centre for Study of Higher Education at Penn State University

References

Heller, D. E. (2002) The policy shift in state financial aid programs. In Smart, J. C. (Ed.) *Higher Education: Handbook of Theory and Research* (Vol. 17, pp. 221–61). New York: Agathon Press.
Organisation for Economic Cooperation and Development (OECD). (2009) *Education at a Glance 2009: OECD Indicators.* Paris: OECD.
Times Higher Education. (2009) The top 200 world universities. Retrieved September 22, 2009 from http://www.timeshighereducation.co.uk/hybrid.asp?typeCode = 243

Acknowledgments

The idea of a book that would try to provide a balanced critique of the introduction of the market into higher education first came to me after I attended a conference on the future of the American public research university at Penn State University in February 2005. It is therefore appropriate that Professor Don Heller, Director of the Center for the Study of Higher Education at Penn State, should have kindly contributed the Foreword. I have benefited greatly from his advice and encouragement and from conversations with other colleagues there.

On the other side of the pond, the chief stimulus came from the review in the UK of the current cap on tuition fees, which is now under way. Colleagues who have provided help and advice here include Jeroen Huisman, David Palfreyman, Gareth Williams, Vaneeta D'Andrea, Tony Bruce, Alan Jenkins, Mick Healey, and Ian McNay. Further afield, they have included Richard Yelland and Richard James. I should also like to thank my contributors, and my editors at Routledge—Sarah Burrows and Alex Sharp—for their patience, courtesy, and advice.

Special thanks are due to five people. My former colleague at Southampton Solent University, Barbara Ebrey, typed much of the text quickly and uncomplainingly. Another former colleague, Lilian Winkvist-Noble, read through the manuscript at a late stage and made some very helpful suggestions. Andy Forbes and her colleagues at Southampton Solent University Library have been enormously efficient in helping me to populate (and annotate) my bibliography. Paulo Charles Pimentel Botas has been everything one could wish for in an assistant, especially in handling the system studies and liaising with the contributors in Chapters 4 to 12. Finally, and most of all, thanks are due to my wife, Josie, for putting up with me during the many months I have laboured over the book.

1

Introduction

ROGER BROWN

> Where effective competition can be created, it is a better means of guiding individual efforts than any other.
>
> (Hayek, 1944: 27, quoted in Marginson, 2004a: 207)

> There is a place for the market, but the market must be kept in its place.
>
> (Okun, 1975: 19, quoted in Kirp, 2005: 127)

The "marketization" (Williams, 1995) of higher education—the application of the economic theory of the market to the provision of higher education—seems unstoppable. Market entry is being liberalized. Tuition fees are being introduced or increased, usually at the expense of state grants to institutions (Salmi, 2009a). Grants for student support (aid) are being supplemented by loans. Institutional rankings and "league tables" to guide student choice are proliferating. Institutions are devoting increasing energy and resources to marketing, branding and customer service. Nor is this phenomenon confined to student education. Much academic research and scholarship is subject to market or "quasi-market" (Le Grand and Bartlett, 1993) coordination as, increasingly, is the recruitment and remuneration of faculty and other staff. Fund raising (seeking donations from alumni and others) is a longstanding feature of the US system and, increasingly, of others. Everywhere institutions are being encouraged or compelled to increase their private funding and reduce their reliance on the taxpayer.

Strong claims are made both by proponents and opponents of markets. Proponents point to a higher level of resourcing than would otherwise be the case bearing in mind the fact that virtually all higher education systems have expanded massively over the past 20–25 years. They also argue that, faced with market competition, institutions will be more effective and responsive in meeting student and other needs, with greater flexibility, innovation and openness to change. Markets provide universities and colleges with the greatest incentive to raise quality and standards. Institutions will also attend to their costs and make the best use of their resources. Altogether, it is said, marketization not only expands the resource "envelope" available to universities and colleges, but also offers society the best value for the resources that it bestows on higher education.

Market opponents point to the increasing stratification of both institutions and the social groups they serve (proponents do not usually claim greater equity but argue that it is the state's job to fix it, not higher education's). They also claim a loss of institutional diversity, an increasingly divided academic community, and detriments to quality and value for money. They also worry about damage to higher education's unwritten "contract" with society, whereby universities and colleges have a wide measure of autonomy in return for the production of various public as well as private goods, sometimes called higher education's "exceptionalism". They descry a concomitant threat to higher education's ability to control, or at least influence, the "academic agenda". Finally, they allege that the marketization of higher education in turn reinforces the marketization of society.

Not surprisingly, there is now a substantial literature on the application of markets to higher education, going back—so far as the author has been able to discover—to the early 1970s (Leslie and Johnson, 1974). Why then is there a need for a fresh study? There are three main reasons.

First, this is a rapidly growing phenomenon. The most recent comparable study (Teixeira et al., 2004) is only six years old. But even in that short time there have been important developments in virtually every major system. Second, with some notable exceptions (e.g., Massy, 2004), writers on the subject tend either to be strongly pro- or anti- in their views, rather than more balanced. Third, many of the existing accounts of marketization rarely make explicit the basis on which they are advocating or deprecating it. There is therefore a need for a book which is not only reasonably up to date but which tries to answer the question: What are the conditions under which market competition can be beneficial to the core activities of universities? and which does so on the basis of a considered view of what a healthy higher education system would look like.

The book accepts the desirability, as well as the reality, of some degree of market competition but outlines—on the basis both of a study of the literature and of experience across a number of major, mostly developed, higher education systems—blended policy responses that could secure both private and public benefits consistent with the best use of society's resources for higher education.

Before going further it may be as well to say a little more of what the book is about:

- The book is essentially a work of scholarship, aiming to provide new insights and understanding on the basis, almost entirely, of existing published work;
- Like most previous accounts, the book focuses mainly on the markets in student, and especially undergraduate, Baccalaureate or "first cycle" education, and academic research and scholarship. This is partly because in most systems these are seen as the core functions of higher education, and partly because (as a consequence) more information is available about the impacts of competition in these cases.

– The book is mainly concerned with the impact of markets on domestic higher education systems. It does not therefore, other than in passing, deal with the markets in international students, faculty or research. These markets are of course far closer to a genuine economic market than most domestic markets. They are also of disproportionate importance to many of the systems we shall be studying (Salmi, 2009a). However to cover these markets properly would require a separate book;

– The book proceeds on the basis that it is appropriate to refer to higher education *systems*. This may be a large assumption to make in the case of the larger countries such as America, Germany or Australia. Nevertheless, as Watson has said: "At some stage, and for some important purposes, every institution is going to rely on the strength and reputation of the system as a whole" (Watson, 2006: 15);[1]

– The book does not go into the wider issues around marketization, and in particular into its suggested causes. For example, for writers such as Shumar (1997), Barber (2007), Bauman (2007) and Lawson (2009), marketization is a function of the overproduction of goods and services by modern capitalism and the consequent necessity of encouraging the citizens of all countries and societies to see themselves as willing consumers. Whilst the author has considerable sympathy with this analysis, it is with the *effects* of marketization on higher education, and the exploitation and mitigation of those effects, that the book is mainly concerned;[2]

– The book respects the views of those (e.g., Zemsky et al., 2005) who argue that higher education, at least in some countries, has always had a commercial side to it so that in this sense marketization is not an entirely new phenomenon. But we consider that what *is* new is the scale of the process and the way in which it appears to be affecting higher education's core functions and values;

– Finally, work on the book was completed before the full effects of the international economic crisis on universities and colleges, and indeed on society and the economy more generally, started to become apparent. However, the events in the financial markets that triggered (if not caused) the crisis would seem to make the book even more topical. Even if not wholly unprecedented, the nature and extent of these market failures should illuminate our understanding of markets in higher education. At the same time, the public expenditure and fiscal consequences will do nothing to reduce the attractiveness, to governments at least, of increased private support for universities. However, the action taken by the authorities in many jurisdictions should also make governments, legislatures, the public and the media less resistant in future to the need for state action to protect the supply of public goods, a key theme of the final chapter.

The book is in three parts.

The first part (Chapters 1–3) introduces the subject, defines "marketization", considers its relevance to higher education, and suggests what, on the basis of the literature to date, appear to be the principal benefits and detriments. The second part (Chapters 4–12) looks at aspects of marketization in nine, mostly mature, systems, all of them developed countries with relatively high participation and expenditure rates: the United States, Australia, the United Kingdom, The Netherlands, Portugal, Germany, Finland, Poland and Japan. The third part (Chapter 13) considers the policy responses that are available if we wish to maximize the benefits and minimize the detriments of markets in higher education. It therefore looks at the shape (structure, governance, composition) of the system; the evaluation and funding of research; the funding of student education; the quality assurance of teaching; and the relationship between research and teaching. The remainder of this Introduction outlines what is meant by "a healthy higher education system".

A Healthy Higher Education System

It is suggested here that a healthy higher education system will be one with the following features:

- It will be valued both for its "intrinsic" qualities in creating, conserving and disseminating knowledge and for its "extrinsic" qualities in serving broader economic, social and cultural goals. Responsibility for determining the system's "academic agenda" is shared between institutions and external stakeholders;
- There is also a balance between the public and private purposes and benefits of higher education;
- There is a balance between the interests of individual institutions and groups of institutions, on the one hand, and the system as a whole, on the other; a balance between institutional autonomy and freedom of action, and integration and common interests;
- There is sufficient diversity of provision to enable the system to respond effectively to new kinds of demands, especially for new kinds of learning opportunities;
- Any significant status or resourcing differentials between individual institutions or groups of institutions are confined to, and justified by, "objective" factors such as local cost differences;
- The student population is broadly representative of the population as a whole;
- The staff are well-qualified, well-motivated and well-managed;
- There is a productive and mutually beneficial relationship between the core activities of institutions: student education and academic research and scholarship;

redistributive expenditure programs, intended to correct market failure, may themselves contain failures because of the inequity of access to them (Wolf, 1993: 85).

Relative Efficiency

Wolf notes that most economists exclude distributional effects from judgments about market success or failure (1993: 28). The main test for distinguishing between the relative effectiveness of markets and non-markets is therefore efficiency. Here the argument, based both on theory and on case studies, is that markets are superior. This is true not only of static efficiency (the ratio of outputs to inputs at any one time) but also of dynamic efficiency (sustaining a higher rate of growth over time due to product or process innovation and better management).

By contrast, non-market activities have inherent inefficiencies deriving from their demand and supply conditions:

> As a consequence, non-market activities . . . often lead to redundant and increasing costs of production. Ancillary functions may be performed that contribute more to pleasing their producers than to accomplishing the purposes for which non-market activities were originally intended.
>
> (Wolf, 1993: 127)

What is of particular interest in the present discussion is the reason for these inefficiencies, namely, the differing processes by which performance is monitored.

Whereas in the non-market domain the main monitors are neither consumers of output nor (usually) rival producers, in the market regime, control over performance is ultimately exercised by consumer behavior and by competing producers whose competition often occurs across product lines as well as within them. The process of controlling costs and quality impinges directly on market output, because the consumer can generally choose to buy less or shift to substitutes, while competing producers can expand their market share by raising output, lowering prices or adding to the substitutes that consumers can choose. The signalling and enforcement mechanism is more direct, impersonal and effective:

> Operation of the market sector's feedback mechanism accounts for the non-pricing efficiencies associated with that sector; and the occurrence of non-market inefficiencies is perhaps equally explained by the *absence* of this mechanism in the non-market sector.
>
> (Wolf, 1993: 130, author's emphasis)

Wolf nevertheless stresses that, the efficiency conclusion notwithstanding, the choice between market and non-market approaches is not between one perfect and one imperfect approach, but between two imperfect approaches.[3]

Market and Non-Market Systems

In the light of this discussion we can now suggest some ideal-type higher education systems for student education.

Table 2.1 Market and non-market models of higher education systems

Market	Non-market
1. *Institutional status*	1. *Institutional status*
Institutions self-governing, independent entities with a high degree of autonomy to determine prices, programs, awards, student numbers, admissions, staff terms and conditions, etc.	Institutions either not independent entities or independent but with little ability to determine prices, etc.
2. *Competition*	2. *Competition*
Low barriers to entry. Lots of competing suppliers. Significant private and/or "for profit" providers offering serious competition to public institutions. Wide student choice. Funding linked to enrollments. Some degree of product/process innovation.	High barriers to entry. Few suppliers or little competition. Few or no private or "for profit" providers. Little student choice. Funding not linked to student numbers. Little product/process innovation.
3. *Price*	3. *Price*
Competition on price of tuition. Fees cover all or a significant proportion of costs and may vary between subjects as well as modes of attendance. Students meet costs of tuition from own or family resources ("cost sharing"). As a result of competition plus price liberalization, considerable variations in price for comparable programs that cannot be explained by local cost factors.	Teaching funded mainly through grants to institutions. No or purely nominal tuition fees. Because of subsidies and/or cross-subsidies, fees bear little or no relation to costs. Fees do not vary between subjects or even modes of attendance. Tuition fees (and sometimes student living costs) heavily subsidized. No cost sharing. Few or no variations in charges for comparable programs.
4. *Information*	4. *Information*
Students make a rational choice based on information about price, quality and availability. Such information plays an important part in their choice of program and supplier.	Limited information about price, quality or availability. Information plays little or no part in student choice of program and supplier.

5. *Regulation*

Facilitates competition whilst providing basic consumer protection. Important role in information provision or brokerage (unless left to market), and dealing with consumer complaints.

6. *Quality*

Ultimately determined by what the market will pay for, which often comes down to what students, employers and the media value (high student entry scores, high postgraduation earnings, etc.). Subsidiary roles for state and academy.

5. *Regulation*

Protects standards and constrains competition that may threaten standards.

6. *Quality*

Usually determined through a combination of state and academic self-regulation, with the state laying down broad frameworks and the key decisions about applying those frameworks being taken by the academic community.

Marketization and Privatization

Before leaving this consideration of concepts, it may be useful to refer to the relationship between marketization—the organization of the supply of higher education "services" on market lines—and privatization—the penetration of private capital, ownership and influence into what were previously publicly funded and owned entities and activities. Conceptually, the two are distinct, indeed the term "quasi-markets" has been coined to describe the organization of the supply of collective services on market lines where no or very little private capital is involved and where the state remains the principal funder and regulator (Le Grand and Bartlett, 1993). Research is a good example. The marketization of research means that instead of being paid as blanket subsidies, funds are allocated to institutions either on the basis of competitive bidding or on the basis of some evaluation of performance, or both.

Nevertheless, a marketized higher education system will be likely to have a significant, perhaps even a dominant, degree of private involvement. In particular, universities and colleges may be privately owned and also geared to producing economic profits for their owners, and the costs of both student education and academic research may be met wholly or largely from private means. More generally, private interests such as business may have an important influence on policy at the system or institutional level (examples include the Committee on Economic Development and the Business Higher Education Forum in the US and the Council for Industry and Higher Education in the UK). It is also possible to see the interests of staff as constituting an important private, as opposed to a collective, public interest in higher education (Calhoun, 2006). Moreover, in practice the application of marketization and privatization, especially the absolute or relative reduction in public financial support and its substitution by private funds, may not be very different.[4]

In fact, both marketization and privatization are often seen as manifestations of a more fundamental shift in public policy making that goes under various terms such as "neo-liberalism". Self (1999) proposed that this ultimately consists of five beliefs (or "dogmas"):

> The "free market" and market-led growth are the principal and overwhelmingly the most important sources of wealth; large incentives are necessary to market efficiency; the wealth created by free markets will trickle down from the successful to benefit all members of society; the market is intrinsically more efficient than government; to gain greater "efficiency", government should be re-designed according to market methods and incentives.
>
> (Self, 1999: 26–28)

As already indicated, it is not proposed here to go into the origins or the merits of these beliefs or the wider literature that has developed around them (for reviews, see Self, 1999; Slaughter and Rhoades, 2004; Marginson, 2007b; Ferlie et al., 2008). What we are concerned with here is what the literature tells us about the *impact* of these beliefs as they translate into policies for higher education. It is to this that we now turn.

Notes

1. Heller (2001: 2) suggests the following tests of student access:

   - Financial: does the student have the financial resources necessary to attend college?
   - Geographic: how far does the potential student have to travel to attend college?
   - Programmatic: is the academic program that the student wants available?
   - Academic: has the student had the proper academic preparation in her or his pre-collegiate years?
   - Cultural/social/physical: Do pre-college students receive the necessary encouragement and support to attend college from parents, families, peers, schools and others? Do some policies (either *de jure* or *de facto*) prohibit or encourage the enrollment of students from particular groups, such as racial minorities, or older, non-traditional college students? Are there physical barriers to attendance, especially for students with a disability that limits their mobility?

2. A number of commentators (e.g., Martin, 2005; McMahon, 2009) add that imperfections in the credit market prevent the optimal private investment in human capital from taking place. Lenders cannot distinguish between good and bad credit risks, cannot tell the difference between high- and low-quality students, and cannot predict which students can, and will, repay educational loans. Without state

intervention there would be serious underinvestment in human capital and inferior levels of economic growth.

3. Wolf also suggests, as non-economic dimensions for comparison, participation and accountability. Participation is the degree to which people, who are affected or are likely to be affected by a given choice between markets and non-markets, participate directly or indirectly in the planning and implementation of the choice. Accountability is the degree to which the outcome of a market or non-market choice is subject to a rigorous process of evaluation and *post hoc* audit concerning its effectiveness and acceptability (1993: 130).

4. Belfield and Levin (2002: 19) distinguish between "external" and "internal" privatization. External privatization refers to the introduction into the market of private institutions whilst internal privatization refers to the increased proportion of institutional revenues from private sources.

3

The Impact of Markets

ROGER BROWN

> Just as capitalist markets generate inequality of wealth in the economy, market coordination in American higher education has tended to exaggerate financial inequality across colleges and universities and encourage social inequality in student access to educational opportunities.
>
> (Geiger, 2004a: 180)

Introduction

Chapter 3 considers what the literature to date suggests about the impact of markets on higher education. It begins by rehearsing the benefits and the limitations of the market model as applied to universities. The most important limitation is the seemingly insuperable difficulty of producing valid, reliable and accessible information about product quality, especially in student education. The corollary is that other, indirect indicators of quality come into play, notably prestige. Since one of higher education's key functions is allocating status, this fuels positional competition in important segments of the market. This in turn creates (or, more likely, reinforces) stratification, not only of institutions but also of the social groups they serve. Other important detriments include a reduction in institutional diversity as homogenizing tendencies in society reinforce those already present in the academy, greater internal differentiation and stratification (of activities, structures and personnel), and risks to quality and value for money. There is also the potential loss of society's trust in universities, stemming from the blurring or removal of the boundaries between academic and commercial work, as universities shift from being communities concerned with maximizing knowledge to being corporations concerned with maximizing revenues. This in turn may call into question society's support for higher education and the legal, financial and cultural benefits for institutions which flow from that.[1]

The Benefits of Markets

Williams (1995: 179) suggested that the movement toward market approaches was based on three main propositions:

- That efficiency is increased when governments buy academic services from producers, or subsidize students to buy them, rather than supplying them directly, or indirectly through subsidy of institutions;
- That as enrollments rise, the private sector must relieve governments of some of the cost burden if acceptable quality is to be obtained;
- That many of the benefits of higher education accrue to private individuals, so criteria of both efficiency and equity are served if students or their families make some contribution toward the costs of obtaining the benefits (cf. Goedegebuure et al., 1994, quoted in Orr, 1997: 46).

Unfortunately, whilst the critiques of markets in higher education are both relatively numerous and specific, the writings in favor are both scarcer and generally less specific. Nevertheless, there does seem to be a measure of agreement on the main benefits.

Efficiency

Market competition makes institutions more aware of their costs. It increases the efficiency with which resources are used, since otherwise institutions are unable to survive, be competitive or obtain the resources and support they need for their activities. This is good in itself but it also makes the resources allocated to higher education go further. Without such pressures, either participation would have had to be constrained or teaching quality would have had to be compromised (assuming some relationship between resourcing and quality). There are cognate arguments on the research side. A particular factor here, which also affects the student curriculum, is the ever increasing growth and specialization of knowledge, for which society may not be able to furnish the necessary resources (Gumport, 2002), and of which the study of higher education itself is a good example. Competition—in the form of performance funding—ensures that research funds are put to the best use, besides stimulating institutions to obtain private support for their research.

Responsiveness

The second set of arguments concerns responsiveness to external stakeholders. Market advocates believe that the market can monitor institutional costs and performance better than non-market mechanisms (the state and the academy). This argument has both "positive" and "negative" aspects. The positive aspect is that universities and colleges tend to be inward-looking, conservative sorts of places (Hefferlin, 1972; cf. Bok, 1990: 19, quoted in Salmi, 2007: 227). Some degree of competition is needed to make them more attentive to the needs, interests and views of the external stakeholders on whose support they depend not only for their resources but also for their relative freedom of action. It may also spur them to a greater degree of innovation. The negative aspect is that without the competitive stimulus, together with some degree of external regulation, institutions will divert their resources to activities that may interest the faculty but which may have little value for society, such as some kinds of research. Competition is also held to provide a stimulus to quality since without it institutions would have no, or less, incentive to improve.

Limitations of the Market Model

It nevertheless seems clear that there are several limitations on the application of the theory of markets to higher education if a healthy system is to be secured:

- Higher education confers both collective (public) and individual (private) advantages. Because of the risk of undersupply, the provision of first cycle education (including student living costs) and academic research are subsidized in most systems;
- Because of the key role which higher education plays as an accreditor of knowledge, especially the knowledge required for the practice of the professions, market entry and competition are regulated in most systems;
- Because of the difficulties of obtaining and disseminating valid, reliable and accessible information about quality, there is a case for a mixed system of regulation, with important roles for the state and the academy, as indeed is the case in most systems;
- Further difficulties arise from the amount of product differentiation and from the difficulty which institutions face, by virtue of the length of the product life cycle, in moving rapidly in response to market signals.

Of these, it is the information difficulty, especially in relation to student education, which appears to present the greatest obstacle to the creation of a proper market.

Information

> The more information that students have on courses and their outcomes, the more they will drive universities to improve.
>
> (Lord Mandelson, quoted in Fearn, 2009)

> Markets cannot discipline price without meaningful information about quality.
>
> (Massy, 2004: 31)

> The perfectly informed customer of economic theory is nowhere to be seen.
>
> (Winston, 1997, quoted in Newman et al., 2004: 91)

The fundamental reason [for the lack of pressure on professors to take teaching seriously] is the difficulty of judging how successful colleges are in helping their students to learn and develop.

(Bok, 2006: 32)

As previously noted, in conventional economic theory, information market failures are usually seen in terms of "asymmetry"—"situations where the amount of information about the characteristics of a good varies in relevant ways between persons" (Weimer and Vining, 1992: 69)—typically, a producer/supplier and a purchaser/consumer. But in higher education, and especially in student education, the problem is less that of unequal access and more that of *no one* having the necessary information. The author has written about this elsewhere (Brown, 2007a) so the argument will just be summarized here (there is a secondary issue about the amount of interest and willingness to use this information in the academy—Brown, 2008; cf. Locke, 2009).

Applied to the provision of student education, the market theory of information would require each of the following conditions to hold:

- It must be possible to produce valid and reliable information about the relative quality of comparable programs and awards in a subject or discipline at different institutions;
- This information must be available to students and other decision makers in a timely, accessible and equitable fashion;
- It must be tailored to the wants, needs, resources and circumstances of each student;
- It must be interpreted and acted upon in a rational manner by that student and/or those advising them;
- It must lead to action by providers to adjust price and/or quality.

Let us consider each of these in turn.

To begin with, to be able to make sound judgments about the comparative quality of programs and awards at different institutions would require:

- The programs to be genuinely comparable in aims, structure, content, learning outcomes, delivery, support, learning environment, resourcing, mission, ethos, etc.;
- The associated awards to involve fully comparable assessment methods, criteria, procedures, outcomes;
- The assessment judgments to be valid, reliable, consistent and fair;
- The students pursuing the program, or who may be interested in doing so, to have comparable starting attainments, aspirations, motivations, learning objectives, etc.

One has only to reflect on these points for a moment to see how unlikely it is that these conditions can be fulfilled in the complex, mass systems that now exist in many countries. In effect, it would require a common curriculum, with tests administered by system examiners, something that is virtually unimaginable (if not highly undesirable) in universities.

But even with this there are problems.

First, the information would need to be provided in advance. Higher education is often referred to as an "experience good", where the consumer is only able to judge the quality of what is being provided as it is being consumed (as opposed to a "search good", the quality of which can be established before it is purchased). In fact, as Weimer and Vining (1992: 75–76) argue, higher education is actually a "*post*-experience good", the effects of which may not appear for many years and may not even be traceable to a particular educational experience (cf. Westerheijden, 2007). Because higher education is an intangible product, and because it involves a judgment-based, customized solution, as in any professional service, it is not always clear to either the teacher or the student what the outcome will be (Lovelock, 1983: 16; cf. Macfarlane, 2007).[2]

Next, the information would have to be provided in a way that was tailored to the distinctive needs and interests of each student, taking account of their background and resources. An independent review of the UK National Student Survey (NSS) emphasized:

> the need to take into account student profiles when making any comparisons using the data, as "raw" figures do not take into account the characteristics of students, their courses and the institutions in which they study may produce at best misleading and at worst invalid measures of teaching.
>
> (Surridge, 2006: 132)

Needless to say, this health warning rarely accompanies the published data (not even on the official website), and of course NSS and other similar exercises are not measures of either teaching or learning (Bótas and Brown, in preparation).

Third, it would need to be balanced, accurate and fair. Here we should note that most of the information would have to be provided by institutions even if it was not published by them. But in a competitive market institutions have powerful incentives to cheat or, at least, to be "economical with the truth" (to use the infamous phrase of the former British Cabinet Secretary, Lord Armstrong). There are many examples in the literature of the lengths to which universities will go to present themselves in the best possible light, indeed this has almost become an industry in its own right (see, e.g., Ehrenberg, 2002; Kirp and Holman, 2003; Watson, 2006; van der Werf, 2009). It is also the case that the present commercial rankings and league tables suit the most prestigious and powerful institutions (Eckel and Couturier, 2006). (Of course, if institutions cheat in this way, they are not on the strongest moral ground when they find their students doing so.)

Next, students and their advisers would need to be able to make judgments on the basis of the information provided and to do so in a rational fashion. Yet there is abundant evidence that even consumers of search goods do not always make rational judgments, and that their behavior is often "adaptive", that is, they behave in accordance with the way they are normally expected to in the circumstances in which they find themselves (Jongbloed, 2003; Hutchings, 2003; Kay, 2003; Vossensteyn, 2005; Stothart, 2007; Cremonini et al., 2008). Certainly there is ample evidence of students acting irrationally (Jongbloed, 2004; Marginson, 2004a). Looking at the decisions made by a wide range of British students, Reay et al. (2005: 58) say that they "found very little of the calculative, individualistic, consumer rationalism that predominates in official texts".[3]

If the student has not acted rationally, it is not clear how an institution can respond to their decision. But even if all the other conditions had been met, and the student had judged rationally, how would the institution know what response to make? Quality is not a science, and what we know about it is greatly outweighed by what we do not.

Finally, all of this assumes that the student is merely a passive recipient of their education, yet it is a commonplace of the pedagogical literature that the student is not only a powerful constituent of their own learning but also of that of others. Even if all the other requirements could be met, it is very hard to see how any system of information can accommodate this dimension.

Some of these difficulties also apply to judgments and information about the quality of research but there are also major differences. There is very often a tangible "product", a publication or an artefact. There is less likely to be a problem of asymmetry: the purchasers are usually better informed (or, less badly informed), and they usually have greater market power. And there does appear to be agreement on the best (or, least unsatisfactory) means of forming judgments, namely, some combination of peer review and bibliometric analysis (for a good critique, see van Raan, 2007).

The Role of Prestige—Institutions and Staff

> Nobody is happy just being what they are.
> (Colorado General Assembly member quoted in Martin, 2005: 17)

> The exclusivity of the elite institutions increases as time passes, as their number and size remain the same, and as the domestic population continues to grow. These trends lead to tournament style results in the income distribution, and the rising income inequality leads to dynastic wealth and dynastic poverty.
> (Martin, 2005: xiv)

The phenomenon that consumers might not have adequate direct information about product/service quality is not unknown in the economic literature. McPherson and Winston (1993: 81) comment that in such circumstances buyers will seek, and producers will try to provide, indirect or symbolic indicators of quality. In higher education, prestige, supported by marketing and conspicuous expenditure, often comes to substitute for quality. This is seen in the Rand Corporation study (Brewer et al., 2002). This found that institutional motivations fell into one of three categories:

- Those institutions seeking to maintain their prestige with other institutions, students and such external stakeholders as state governments, business and alumni;
- Those seeking to acquire such prestige;
- Those seeking to build a reputation for successfully meeting the needs of students and other potential "customers".

The choice of strategy—prestige or reputation—was determined by the institution's starting point, its ownership, its governance and the markets where it was active. Where institutional strategy was determined by the faculty, the institution tended to seek prestige. Where strategy was determined by outside owners, or where there were very clear market signals, the institution sought reputation (Eckel, 2008: 175 prefers "effectiveness"). Dill (2003: 148) suggests that in the student market, prestigious and prestige-seeking institutions invest in improving admissions selectivity, lowering acceptance/yield rates and student consumption benefits (dormitories, eating facilities, fibre-optic networks) whilst institutions seeking reputation invest in courses to serve the local business community, convenient course scheduling and student services. Other strategies to enhance prestige include renaming the institution and creating "honors colleges" to attract higher scoring students (Newman et al., 2004: 14–15).

Massy (2003: 23) refers to a subsequent study by the Pennsylvania Institute for Research on Higher Education covering 1,200 institutions (the Rand study covered 26). This found that about half the nation's universities appeared to enjoy or be seeking prestige even though this is largely pointless because such prestige is by definition limited in quantity, and the really prestigious institutions have a huge "lead" over the rest: the elite tends to remain the elite and success breeds success (cf. Bok, 2003; Kirp, 2003b; Astin and Oseguera, 2004; Marginson, 2007b; Rhoades, 2005; Sweitzer et al., 2009; Geiger, 2009). Examining the 33 institutions serving the Atlanta market, Toma (2009: 12) found that nearly every institution was aiming to "move to the next level".

There are several points to be emphasized here.

The first is the key role of the faculty in determining policy, at least in "not for profit" institutions. Massy (2003: 97–101) speaks of the "academic ratchet", the steady, irreversible shift of faculty allegiance away from the goals of a given institution toward those of an academic specialty. Calhoun (2006: 36) argues that:

> The academic self-understanding—the class-consciousness of profes-sors—has inhibited adequate recognition of major transformations in uni-versities, higher education and the production of knowledge, and has stood in the way of focusing attention on the public purposes of universities—which are in fact those most likely to secure legitimate academic values for the future.

Institutional leaders are also culpable:

> While many leaders within public higher education decry the perceived disinvestment in their public mission, they nonetheless enjoy the idea of gaining greater autonomy. Furthermore, many have themselves become enamoured of the non-public revenue streams that are becoming increas-ingly available to them and with which they can do non-public things.
>
> (Longanecker, 2005: 68)

The second is the importance of graduate training in the formation of faculty. In many systems, future faculty obtain their higher qualifications, usually PhDs, at more prestigious, usually "research intensive" institutions. They then take posi-tions at less prestigious ones. Many then devote their efforts either to returning to their alma mater or making the place where they are working as much like their alma mater as possible. This emphasis on status and hierarchy (Eckel and Couturier, 2006) helps to explain the seemingly inevitable phenomenon of "aca-demic drift" (we will consider this again when we look at institutional diversity).

The third is the crucial part that, partly as a consequence of the informational difficulties with education, performance in research plays in the accumulation of institutional, departmental and professional prestige:

> Although the gains to society from high quality university research are incalculable, they have been accompanied by huge expenditure of effort and resources on poorer quality research, seriously detracting from the central role of teaching by reducing both the time and creativity faculty devote to teaching, undervaluing those institutions whose principal role is teaching and particularly undervaluing those whose chief role is teaching the least advantaged.
>
> (Newman et al., 2004: 52; cf. Duderstadt and Womack, 2003; Sperber, 2005; Zemsky et al., 2005; and many others)

Calhoun (2006: 25) also echoes this and points to the overproduction of PhDs (at least in relation to the academic job market) as another symptom of the priority given to research. Volkwein and Sweitzer (2006: 143) found that even at US liberal arts colleges, which are teaching oriented, publications per full-time faculty correlated positively with prestige.

The fourth is the very close association between prestige and wealth. Watson and Bowden pointed to the very high correlation (better than 0.9) between an institution's wealth (as denoted by gross income per full-time equivalent [FTE] student) and its *Times League Table* position (Watson and Bowden, 2002; subsequent calculations by the author confirm that these correlations persist over time). Geiger (2004a: 168) and others (e.g., Volkwein and Sweitzer, 2006) found the same in the US (the *US News and World Report* rankings actually reward high-spending institutions). Geiger also points out that the disparities have increased: the private institutions have increased their resources at the expense of the public ones, and the resource-rich institutions are the ones that have gained the most (2004a: 179–80; cf. Winston, 2000 and Geiger, 2004b). Calhoun (2006: 25) notes that the availability of elite status actually depends on the dramatic inequalities of funding available to institutions at different places in the hierarchy (2006: 32).

The Role of Prestige—Students and Employers

> We see a national obsession with becoming the best by attending the best.
> (Volkwein and Grunig, 2005: 256)

However, it is not only institutions and academics that are playing the prestige game. Many students are keen on attending prestigious institutions, and many employers are keen to recruit there (Ehrenberg, 2002 and many others). Moreover, as Frank has shown, they are able, or at least encouraged, to do so by the information revolution that has made us more aware of product differences than ever before, whilst at the same time putting us in direct touch with the world's leading suppliers (Frank and Cook, 1995; Frank, 1999; Frank, 2007). Not only do these firms reinforce the increased demand for elite credentials, they behave in the same way as elite universities. They need the graduates of elite institutions as much as those graduates need them. Moreover, the more applicants they attract, the better they do: "The market for higher education, always a winner-takes-all market, has become perhaps the quintessential example of such a market" (Frank, 1999: 9).[4]

Morley and Aynsley (2007) demonstrate a similar phenomenon in the UK. Watson (2008: 11) points out that if employers are choosing institutions on the basis of reputation, rather than educational quality, it is rational for students to do so too.

Status

We come now to what may be the nub of the matter: status. When people write about the functions of universities they usually refer to student education, academic research and scholarship, and services to third parties ("service", "engagement", "knowledge transfer", etc.). But universities also allocate status through the granting of credentials: this could even be described as the "fourth function" of higher education (it is mainly done through student education but research plays an important role in generating the knowledge on which such credentialing is based). Slaughter and Leslie (1997: 4) comment that faculty could even be regarded as the "paramount profession" because they control the academic entry qualifications on which entry to most professions is based.

Collins (2002: 37) notes the enormous expansion of credentials that has taken place in American higher education, with students proceeding to higher and higher levels of education, so that a Master's degree today is "worth" what a Baccalaureate degree was yesterday. (Similarly, Shumar, 1997, points out that whereas previously a PhD might have been sufficient qualification for an academic post, what is now needed is a PhD with publications.)

In principle, it would be possible to restrict the numbers being credentialed at each level but in practice this is difficult:

> Our current period of credential inflation has gone along with several other kinds of inflation: grade inflation, admissions inflation (students multiplying the number of schools to which they apply), recommendation inflation (as increasingly glowing rhetoric is used to install the merits of students and job candidates), CV inflation (as academic job candidates add more and more details to their official accomplishments). Our prevailing cultural ethos is for teachers to treat students sympathetically, to try to get them through what they recognise as a competitive grind. The ethos of democracy and equality fits with the structure of self-reinforcing inflation, and of course the students are paying handsomely for the privilege. The alternative of dealing with massive competition by raising standards is much more difficult in these circumstances.
>
> (Collins, 2002: 38)

If universities were merely profit-oriented enterprises they would not be a good investment: "But the credential-producing economy is a prestige economy, closer to the structure of the potlatch than that of a classical laissez-faire market" (Collins, 2002: 38).

Competition for status—positional competition—may be unavoidable as increased economic activity leads to crowding and redundancy (Self, 1999: 77). It becomes socially significant when it takes place in an economic context, when the market economy becomes the medium for such competition through variable tuition and aid, institutional competition for both public and private funding, the introduction of "for profit" providers, and officially sponsored (or condoned) performance indicators and rankings.

Given the difficulties in comparing quality, as well as the market and political power wielded by the top ranked institutions and the constituencies they serve (who include many in influential positions in government, the professions and the media), one seemingly inevitable corollary of marketization is greater stratification as elite institutions seek to differentiate themselves as "world-class". However:

> At the bottom end of the market, the workings of status competition are different. Institutions must compete hard to attract students to fill their places and secure revenues: and their success is always provisional and contestable but these institutions do not receive full recognition of the quality of good programmes. In a status market, their attempts to improve the quality of their teaching are over-determined by their low status. Meanwhile, intermediate institutions, combining scarce high-value spaces with low-value access places, find it difficult to move up the ladder because of limits to the number of high-prestige producers.
>
> (Marginson, 2004b: 190)

This phenomenon is not confined to America or Australia. In Britain:

> Marketing and advertising of colleges threaten to produce a system of highly prestigious sought-after institutions in high demand, a second layer of less illustrious institutions doing their best to imagine themselves illustrious, and a huge number of institutions using all the marketing techniques they can get their hands on to sell their product to a consuming public.
>
> (Reay et al., 2005: 140; cf. Shumar, 1997: 134)[5]

This competitive advantage ultimately boils down to a new version of the "Three Rs": resources (especially income from endowments and donations), reputation and research. The position is well summarized by Winston:

> Competition at the top is heavily positional . . . the bottom line for any school is its access to the donative wealth that buys quality and position. Several authors have described the conflict between individual and social rationality and the wasteful dynamics of positional markets. Essentially, the notion is that the players become trapped in a sort of upward spiral, an arms race, seeking relative position.
>
> (Winston, 1999: 30; cf. Calhoun, 2006: 26)

This donative wealth of course not only gives certain institutions a direct advantage but also acts as a "barrier to entry" to competition at that level. Geiger necessarily precede applied research. This has been exemplified by the National Institutes for Health as medical substances and devices, along with biotechnology, became key industries in the new economy. Similar trends can be seen with Research Council funding in Britain (cf. Powell and Owen-Smith, 2002; Reich, 2004; Calhoun, 2006).

Slaughter and Rhoades also see the development of new "circuits of knowledge" as a threat to the control of the academy over what is taught. Just as knowledge no longer moves primarily within scientific/professional/scholarly networks, teaching is no longer the province of faculty members who work with students in classrooms and are connected to wider realms of knowledge through their departments and disciplinary associations. Courseware such as Blackboard and WebCT link faculty to electronic platforms that standardize teaching across institutions, creating new circuits of knowledge that are more accountable to administrators than disciplinary associations. *The Chronicle of Higher Education* carried an article in September 2008 about university concerns over their growing dependence on Blackboard for course management software (Young, 2008).

The whole question of the extent to which the academy can retain control over the academic agenda—crudely, what is to be taught and researched, and how—is closely bound up with the wider issue of the relationship between higher education and society and in particular the relationship of trust which exists between society and the academy. This is an issue to which we shall shortly return.

Quality

> If funding follows the student, this will introduce a greater degree of competition into the system and drive up standards.
>
> (Boris Johnson MP, UK Shadow Minister for Higher Education, 2005)

> No reliable method yet exists that allows students to determine where they will learn the most. Since applicants are generally hard-put to know just how much they are really learning, let alone how much they can expect to learn at a school they have never seen, they do not make enlightened choices. They rarely possess either the time or the information to explore all the promising options available to them and usually have only a limited basis for considering the options they do consider. Under these conditions, competition does not necessarily cause good instruction to drive out bad. Instead, students often flock to courses with superficial appeal or to institutions with established reputations even though the education they receive is only mediocre.
>
> (Bok, 2003: 161)

Bearing in mind the difficulties of defining quality, what, based on the literature, can we say about the impact of markets on quality? In principle, it is argued, greater competition should improve quality as suppliers respond to customers' wants and needs to improve their standing and resources. However the literature points in different directions.

As already noted, there appears to be wide agreement that increased competition has made universities more responsive, more flexible, and more "customer aware", as well as more efficient in their use of resources. Whether this has raised quality, in terms of enhancing students' educational experiences and achievements (in so far as they can be descried), is a separate question. There are in fact suggestions in the literature that marketization or, to be quite accurate, marketization with its associated policies of privatization and the relative reduction of public funding (Vincent-Lancrin, 2009), may have had a *negative* impact on the quality of student education.

These suggestions include:

- A reduction in the amount of student learning due to a reduction in the "volume" of the curriculum, a shorter academic year, less contact with lecturers and tutors, heavier academic workloads, larger teaching groups, higher student-staff ratios, more students working in term-time, etc. (White, 2007; Callender, 2008). This partly reflects resourcing pressures, partly the greater priority given to research (in the US, the proportion of institutional expenditure devoted to instruction has steadily declined);
- Lower levels of retention, longer time to graduate, etc. though these may also be a function of expansion and lower selectivity (Ehrenberg, 2006; Shireman, 2009);
- Greater pressure on pass rates, grade inflation (Shumar, 1997; Johnson, 2003; Sperber, 2005; Hunt, 2008) especially at the most prestigious institutions (Bowen, 2004a; Geiger, 2004b; Yorke, 2008), increased plagiarism and other forms of cheating. Such cheating is not confined to academic work once a student has enrolled: Marcus (2008) describes how there is growing evidence of students and parents cheating in the American admissions process;
- A declining level of trust between students and staff seen in increasing student complaints and even misbehaviour in the form of violence, harassment, public humiliation and rudeness as well as accusations of unfairness and lack of professionalism (Lee, 2006; Tahir, 2007; Attwood, 2009b). This may reflect an increasing mismatch between the priorities of the faculty and those of the students, with the former increasingly geared to research and publication whilst the latter emphasize learning and credentials (Levine, 2005);
- (As already noted) increased resort to temporary and part-time lecturers and tutors, including graduate students, many of them neither properly trained nor committed to the institution (Kirp, 2005; Ehrenberg, 2006). This is often due to "research active" faculty being "bought out" of their

Britain, is the best use of society's resources. A particular case here is the seemingly endless rise in the cost of tuition in the US: "The Consumer Price Index has increased 119 percent since 1980 while public university tuition has increased 543 percent, or more than four times the increase in general prices" (Heller, 2007: 37).

This has increased the relative cost of higher education for all households, at a time when a college education is even more essential for high earnings and a prestigious career. But because family income inequality has also been growing, higher education has become still more expensive for those from poorer families:

> For those at the 20th percentile of all households, those with incomes of $18,000 in 2003, the proportion of income required to pay public university tuition increased from 12 percent of income in 1967 to 30 percent in 2003. In contrast, for families at the 95th percentile, the proportion of income required grew from 2 percent to only 3.5 percent.
>
> (Heller, 2007: 37)

There do not appear to have been any compensating improvements in quality. There have been various initiatives in Congress to legislate to control tuition rises, culminating (for the moment) in the reauthorized Higher Education Act provisions requiring the Education Department to publish an annual "watch list" of institutions with the highest percentage increases in tuition fees, though there are reported to be serious doubts as to how effective this is likely to be (Kelderman, 2009).

A number of explanations have been put forward for the increases, but one definite contributor is increased competition, bearing in mind the fact that (as we have already seen) in a positional market price acts as a signal for quality. Instead of increased competition leading to a lowering of prices, prices increase to "what the market will bear" (Hirsch, 1976; Frank and Cook, 1995; Winston, 1999; Frank, 1999; Kay, 2003; Frank, 2007). In the US, the leading private institutions are able to exploit their status, location (usually in more prosperous areas), and wealth. The leading public institutions have had little choice to follow them in raising tuition and becoming more selective and less "local". This competition results in higher net prices (the full or "sticker" fee after deducting institutional aid).

Other contributory factors include increased demand (bearing in mind the continuing gap in earnings between high school and university graduates); the fact that (as we saw earlier) the supply of places, at least at the most selective institutions, has not grown in line with demand; increased financial aid (though it hasn't kept pace with fees); increased costs (partly reflecting the increased importance of research); declining State appropriations; and the generally weak oversight that enables heads of institutions to increase their remuneration by significant amounts each year almost irrespective of the performance of their institutions (for a further discussion, see Brown, 2009a).[9]

Taking quality and value for money together, Dill has summarized the position thus:

> Because the new competitive market is characterized by inadequate and inappropriate information, an ambiguous conception—"academic prestige"—comes to represent academic quality in the public mind, which can lead to a price-quality association that undermines productive efficiency. The distorting influence of prestige in both the US and UK markets means that the educational costs of elite universities provide a "price umbrella" for the rest of the system and present spending targets for less elite institutions that wish to compete by raising their prices (Massy, 2004). Competitive markets thereby encourage an academic "arms race" for prestige amongst all institutions, which rapidly increases the costs of higher education and devalues the improvement of student learning. As noted in both the US and UK, an unregulated academic market can lead to a situation in which no university constituency—students, faculty members or administrators— has a compelling incentive to assure academic standards. This is a recipe for a classic and significant market failure in which the rising social costs of higher education are not matched by equivalent social benefits (Teixeira et al., 2004).
>
> (Dill, 2007: 67)[10]

Universities' Relationship with Society

> The classic justification for the non-profit status of educational institutions is that it redresses information asymmetry between buyers and sellers. Because consumers cannot adequately monitor the quality of educational services, they prefer dealing with institutions they can trust not to take advantage of them to make a profit. But maximising revenue now looks a good deal like making a profit. Private universities now engage in such deceptive practices as awarding less aid to early admission students or front-loading the first year of aid packages (McPherson and Shapiro, 1998). Students in the aggregate may gain greater wages through these arrangements, but each student must fend for themselves. Trust in this relationship can no longer be assumed.
>
> (Geiger, 2004a: 171)

> If trust is only defined by the market, once trust is lost by the state in its relationships with higher education, then the role of higher education in creatively questioning, and thus shaping, the nature of the state is also in danger of being lost.
>
> (Gibbs, 2001: 90; cf. Molesworth et al., 2009: 285)

The final impact of marketization concerns universities' relationship with the rest of society. Ramaley (2005) is amongst a number of authors who argue that marketization is a threat to the public role of higher education either because it is hostile to the notion of the public good or because it sees the public good as being achieved only through the production of private goods. But there is a still wider issue.

We have already noted that in many systems universities enjoy a high degree of autonomy in return for the crucial role they play in certifying knowledge (especially the knowledge needed for professional practice). For the same reasons, institutions (public and private) often benefit from tax breaks and other benefits. But if the boundaries between academic and commercial activities are breaking down, so that universities and colleges are increasingly acting as commercial entities and their public mission is becoming obscured (Reich, 2004; cf. Longanecker, 2005), can these continuing concessions be justified?

Newman et al. (2004: 53) emphasize that public higher education benefits many more citizens of the state than those attending the institutions or receiving services from extension services. Research shows that there is a social return to higher education that includes increased income for non-college graduates, increased state tax revenues, increased inter-generational mobility and lower welfare costs. If a high tuition policy for public higher education reduces the fraction of the population going on to and completing college, everyone will be worse off. McMahon (2009: 30) estimates that the social (i.e., non-private) benefits amount to 52 percent of the total benefits.[11]

The Impact of Marketization—Conclusion

It may be useful to summarize this somewhat compressed discussion of the literature on the impact of marketization.

On the plus side, a number of writers (e.g., Massy, 2004) draw attention to the stimulus which marketization provides to increased efficiency, responsiveness to customers (though some customers are more equal than others and there can also be a tendency to put institutional interests, in building revenues and prestige, ahead of those of their customers), and innovation and revenue diversification compared with a government controlled, non-market system. Massy argues that, for the reasons already considered in the earlier discussion of non-market systems, market systems will be superior to others in motivating productivity improvement and in responding to changes in supply and demand, and are also capable of doing so in ways that further the public good. However:

> The markets for higher education as currently constituted fail in certain crucial respects. Universities tend to value faculty for their own sake, which inhibits technology-based productivity improvement. They honour the perceived "property rights" of faculty, which inhibits growth by

substitution. They do not resist mission drift, which encourages faculty to substitute research for educational tasks, to the detriment of students. They under-invest in the provision of information about education quality, which forces the market to rely on surrogates that serve the interests of providers far more than those of consumers.

(Massy, 2004: 31)

For a writer like William Bowen, who is by no means uncritical of the market, the basic American model of a decentralized, variegated system has served the country well. A willingness to use market mechanisms, healthy respect for freedom of expression and critical inquiry, and a pluralistic set of decision makers and funding sources together generate more resources and innovation than a "monolithic" system would produce. The resultant diverse and highly competitive structure has allowed American higher education to avoid the pitfalls of forced homogeneity and associated influences that are found in many countries. Different kinds of public and private institutions, costing different amounts of money to operate and attend, serve the varied needs (and interests) of multiple clienteles. The result is a system that is both more effective and more efficient than one that is centrally planned and controlled (Bowen et al., 2005: 248; cf. Ben-David, 1977).

But there is another side to the picture. The negative, or potentially negative, impacts of markets highlighted in the literature include increased stratification (of both institutions and social groups); reduced diversity (as the push for prestige outside the institutions by students and employers reinforces the pursuit of prestige within the academy: the pathology of the market reinforcing the pathology of the academy?); greater internal differentiation of activities, structures and personnel; risks to quality; and poorer value for money as resources are diverted into wasteful positional competition. But the biggest threat to liberal higher education appears to come from the increasing interpenetration of the values and practices of business and commerce. These are already blurring the boundaries of the academy and pose a potentially serious threat to its long standing and generally beneficial (for both sides) relationship with society.

In the third part of this book we consider what policy responses might enable us to accommodate these pressures, so that both the institutions and society can capture the benefits of market competition whilst avoiding or minimizing the detriments. But before doing so we review the extent and impact of marketization in nine mostly developed higher education systems.

Notes

1. It should be noted that the largest proportion of this literature is from, and about, the US, followed by Australia and the UK. This reflects the fact that America has

the largest and historically most successful system, as well as the greatest experience of marketization (Vincent-Lancrin, 2009).

2. People investing in human capital through a purchase of higher education don't know what they're buying—and wouldn't and can't know what they have bought until it is far too late to do anything about it (Winston, 1999: 15).

3. Jongbloed (2006: 25) comments:

> If individuals are fundamentally rational and the problems are [uncertainty, imperfect information], the potential role for policy would be to try to address these market imperfections by helping students make the decisions they want. If, on the other hand, students are fundamentally irrational then giving them more information or eliminating market imperfections will not necessarily improve outcomes. In the latter case there may not be a need to strengthen consumer choice in higher education, and it might be better to, for example, let educational authorities offer the programmes they deem best for students rather than let student preference drive programme selection.

4. "Winner-takes-all" markets are those where small differences in performance, real or perceived, translate into large differences in reward. Frank argues that such markets used to be confined to relatively rare instances such as opera singers, but the information revolution means that we can instantly discover who or what is the top performer in any market so that the rest are merely also-rans.

5. Zemsky (2005: 287) notes:

> What the faculty and staff of both private and public institutions have learned is that in the end there is really no market advantage accorded to institutions that provide extra-quality education . . . What happens in this market is not quality but rather competitive advantage.

6. There is a vast literature on this subject, so vast that indeed that (at least without going mad) no one can possibly have read everything that has been written. Amongst useful recent summaries, see Dill and Soo, 2005; van Dyke, 2005; Yorke and Longden, 2005; Usher and Savino, 2006; Brown, 2006; Marginson, 2007a; Salmi and Saroyan, 2007; Sadlak and Liu Nian Cai, 2007; Locke et al., 2008; Fidler and Parsons, 2008; Hazelkorn, 2008; Kivisto and Holtta, 2008; Kehm and Stensaker, 2009.

7. Rhoades (2007: 123) argues that:

> More public research universities would do better to seek strategic, sustainable and synergistic niches. The common choices being made by public research universities are in significant ways compromising us socially (in the students we serve), economically (in the investments we are making in particular research markets) and politically (in the external employers we are connecting with).

> He goes on to suggest student, research and employer markets that could offer alternatives to the limited range of strategies currently being pursued by institutions.

8. Slaughter and Rhoades conceptualize universities as shifting from a "public good knowledge/learning regime" to an "academic capitalist knowledge/learning regime" (2004: 1). The former valued knowledge as a public good on which the citizenry has claims, the latter construes knowledge as a private good, valued especially for creating streams of high-technology products that generate profits as they flow through global markets. However, the newer regime does not necessarily displace the old: the two co-exist, intersect and overlap.

9. Geiger (2004a: 179) points out that, rather than expand their enrollments, the elite privates choose to use their additional revenues to build up quality (by attracting better qualified students) and financial assets. He also notes that where price competition between such institutions exists, it takes the form of differential pricing for individual students rather than a general bidding down of prices.

10. Cf. Massy (2004: 31):

> In the US, elite institutions exploit peer effects and price-quality associations to boost their own spending and provide a pricing umbrella for other universities and, indeed, for state governments that wish to shift spending priorities away from higher education. Worst of all, information shortfalls prevent the market's invisible hand from driving incentives for quality improvement. We are caught in a vicious circle that produces an arms race in spending without regard to educational value added. This encourages mission drift, which actually inhibits education quality improvement.

11. McMahon also comments on the way in which higher education has turned away from the more general needs of society toward its own preoccupations: attracting students, focusing on internal management issues and preoccupied with competition with other institutions (2009: 287). The author has noted how media reporting of higher education, at least in Britain, has moved away from looking at the performance of the system as a whole to focusing on the standing and performance of individual institutions, with seemingly endless discussion of whether Oxford or Cambridge has now become Britain's "top university" even though neither institution is in any way representative of the British system.

Just as material resources and socioeconomic differences constrain the college choice process, informational asymmetries can sharply divide students. For example, because educational quality proves difficult to assess, students tend to use admissions selectivity as a proxy for educational quality. If an HEI admits a relatively low percentage of its applicants, students generally perceive the HEI as a high-quality provider (Karabel and Astin, 1975; Litten and Hall, 1989; Trow, 1984). Perceptions of institutional quality prove a key dimension along which students define their postsecondary options. Most students engage in "self-selection," the process of applying only to institutions to which they believe they both may gain admission and can afford to attend (Hossler and Litten, 1993; Hossler et al., 1999; McDonough, 1997). Such a practice assumes the ability to judge accurately both the HEI's admission standards and the student's own qualifications.

Students generally glean information about colleges and universities from a variety of sources, including high school counselors, parents, and publications that HEIs generate about themselves (Paulsen, 1990). Yet neither these resources nor the knowledge they convey is evenly distributed among students. Low-income, black, and/or Latino students often have few reliable sources of information on which to draw. Further, the sources of data to which they have access are often high school counselors who have little time to invest in shaping students' postsecondary aspirations (McDonough, 1997; McDonough and Calderone, 2006). As a result, low-income families are generally far less able than affluent families to estimate either the costs or student aid support available for attending a particular HEI (Grodsky and Jones, 2007). In addition, and perhaps as a result, parents of such students therefore may pressure their children to attend an HEI that is close to home rather than an institution matched to that student's academic ability (Lopez-Turley, 2006).

Discussion—The Interaction of Imperfect Competition and Constrained Choice

A discussion of markets presumes a fair basis for competition. This presumption, and its correlate assumption of fairness to different competitors, provides markets with credibility as mechanisms for the allocation of resources (Apple, 2001). However, stratification and imperfect competition characterize both the supply and the demand side of the student enrollment marketplace. Winston (2004) provided one possible interpretation of this stratification by suggesting that enrollment positions may be allocated meritocratically. If rich institutional resources are paired with high-ability students, then spending on higher education may efficiently invest resources in students for whom those resources are likely to yield the greatest return. In this case, stratification would serve the public good. The disproportionate subsidy afforded to high-ability students would yield graduates who translate the benefits of a costly education into innovations, broadened tax bases, and educated voters.

Winston advanced this idea cautiously, and with good reason. His model of matching high-ability students with disproportionately larger subsidies presumes that students develop choice sets that include HEIs from varied deciles. When the realities of the higher education marketplace are juxtaposed with what we know about the college choice process, a pattern emerges that is sharply at variance with this happy reconciliation. Students with more substantial material and informational resources are less likely to be price-sensitive or geographically bounded than are their low-income peers. These behavioral differences make well-to-do students considerably more likely to find and consider HEIs that offer generous general subsidies. Similar patterns obtain with regard to organizations. The most impoverished colleges offer such substantial price discounts that they may undermine the very tuition revenue on which they depend (Redd, 2000). By contrast, the most affluent HEIs have access both to a broader range of revenue options and to more qualified students than they can admit. These institutions therefore may limit student aid awards to fewer individuals. Placed alongside one another, these two patterns reveal the imperfectly competitive nature of the student enrollment marketplace. Low-income students employ the most constrained choice sets, which are dominated by HEIs offering lower general subsidies, while their more affluent peers choose among HEIs that offer more generous general subsidies.

We should emphasize that students do make real choices and that many students make choices at odds with our model. The US market provides ample room for agency and choice. As DesJardins and Toutkoushian (2005) suggest, a student who elects to stay close to home and/or to apply to a less selective HEI may do so for reasons that maximize personal gain, measured broadly, even if they do not maximize prestige or long-term earning potential. Indeed, low-income students in the 1990s pursued postsecondary education in greater numbers than in any previous decade. Rates of attendance rose despite rapidly rising tuition prices (Heller, 2001).

This acknowledgment of the real role of individual agency in the marketplace returns us to the thesis of our essay. Our discussion in this chapter is less about social determinism than it is about the complex reality of the US higher education system, and the products and consequences of its multiple markets. Patterns among students and institutions suggest that the marketplace of American higher education is characterized by informational and material constraints linked to material resources, not by the featureless plain of opportunity assumed in a perfectly competitive marketplace. US higher education markets exist as a product of the choices institutions and students make within particular situated contexts rather than in a vacuum in which they seek only to maximize utility. Ignoring the segmentation and imperfections of these markets may cause us to ignore the fact that these choices have consequences that undermine the productive, efficient nature of our higher education system.

References

Apple, M. W. (2001) Comparing neo-liberal projects and inequality in education. *Comparative Education,* 37(4): 409–23.

Baum, S. (2001) *Higher Education Dollars and Sense: A Framework for Campus Conversations.* New York: The College Entrance Examination Board.

Breneman, D. W., Doti, J. L. & Lapovsky, L. (2001) Financing private colleges and universities: the role of tuition discounting. In Paulsen, M. B. & Smart, J. C. (Eds) *The Finance of Higher Education: Theory, Research, Policy, and Practice,* New York: Agathon Press.

Brewer, D. J., Gates, S. M. & Goldman, S. A. (2002) *In Pursuit of Prestige: Strategy and Competition in U.S. Higher Education.* New Brunswick, NJ: Transaction Publishers.

Cheslock, J. J. (2006) Applying economics to institutional research on higher education revenues. In Toutkoushian, R. K. & Paulsen, M. B. (Eds) *Applying Economics to Institutional Research,* San Francisco, CA: Jossey-Bass.

The College Board (2008) *Trends in College Pricing: 2008.* Washington, DC: The College Board.

Desjardins, S. & Toutkoushian, R. (2005) Are students really rational? the development of rational thought and its application to student choice. In Smart, J. C. (Ed.) *Higher Education: Handbook of Theory and Research, Vol. XX.* New York: Springer.

Grodsky, F. & Jones, M. T. (2007) Real and imagined barriers to college entry: perceptions of cost. *Social Science Research,* 36(1): 745–66.

Hearn, J. C. (1991) Academic and nonacademic influences on the college destinations of 1980 high school graduates. *Sociology of Education,* 64(3): 158–71.

—— (1984) The relative roles of academic, ascribed, and socioeconomic characteristics in college destinations. *Sociology of Education,* 57(1): 22–30.

Heller, D. E. (2001) Trends in the affordability of public colleges and universities: the contradiction of increasing prices and increasing enrollment. In Heller, D. E. (Ed.) *The States and Public Higher Education Policy.* Baltimore, MD: The Johns Hopkins University Press.

Hossler, D. & Gallagher, K. S. (1987) Studying student college choice: a three phase model and the implications for policy makers. *College and University,* 23(3): 207–21.

Hossler, D., Kuh, G. D. & Olsen, D. (2001) Finding fruit on the vines: using higher education research and institutional research to guide institutional policies and strategies. *Research in Higher Education,* 42(2): 211–21.

Hossler, D. & Litten, H. (1993) *Mapping The Higher Education Landscape.* New York: College Entrance Examination Board.

Hossler, D., Schmit, J. & Vesper, N. (1999) *Going to College: How Social, Economic, and Educational Factors Influence the Decisions Students Make.* Baltimore, MD: The Johns Hopkins University Press.

Hovey, H. A. (1999) *State Spending for Higher Education in the Next Decade: the Battle to Sustain Current Support.* San Jose, CA: National Center for Public Policy and Higher Education.

Karabel, J. & Astin, A. W. (1975) Social class, academic ability, and college "quality." *Social Forces,* 53(3): 381–98.

Karen, D. (2002) Changes in access to higher education in the United States. *Sociology of Education,* 75(3): 191–210.

Kinzie, J., Palmer, M., Hayek, J., Hossler, D., Jacob, S. A. & Cummings, H. (2004) *Fifty Years of Educational Choice: Social, Political, and Institutional Influences on the Decision-Making Process* (New Agenda Series 5, no. 3). Indianapolis, IN: Lumina Foundation for Education.

Leslie, L. & Johnson, G. P. (1974) The market model and higher education. *The Journal of Higher Education,* 45(1): 1–20.

Levine, A. & Nidiffer, J. (1995) *Beating the Odds: How the Poor Get to College.* San Francisco: Jossey-Bass Publishers.

Li, D. (2008) Degree attainment of undergraduate student borrowers in four-year institutions: a multilevel analysis. *Journal of Student Financial Aid,* 37(3): 5–19.

Litten, L. H. & Hall, A. E. (1989) In the eyes of our beholders: some evidence on how high-school students and their parents view quality in colleges. *Journal of Higher Education,* 60(3): 302–24.

Litten, L. H., Sullivan, D. & Brodigan, D. L. (1983) *Applying Market Research in College Admissions.* New York: The College Entrance Examination Board.

Lopez-Turley, R. N. (2006) When parents want children to stay home for college. *Research in Higher Education,* 47(7): 823–46.

McDonough, P. M. (1997) *Choosing Colleges: How Social Class and Schools Structure Opportunity.* Albany, NY: State University of New York Press.

McDonough, P. M. (1994) Buying and selling higher education: the social construction of the college applicant. *The Journal of Higher Education,* 65(4): 427–46.

McDonough, M. P. & Calderone, S. (2006) The meaning of money: perceptual differences between college counselors and low-income families about college costs and financial aid. *American Behavioral Scientist,* 49(12): 1703–18.

McPherson, M. S. & Schapiro, M. O. (1998) *The Student Aid Game: Meeting Need and Rewarding Talent in American Higher Education.* Princeton, NJ: Princeton University Press.

Monks, J. (2000) The returns to individual and college characteristics: evidence from the National Longitudinal Survey of Youth. *Economics of Education Review,* 19(3): 279–89.

Paulsen, M. B. (1990) *College Choice: Understanding Student Enrollment Behavior.* Washington, DC: The George Washington University.

Paulsen, M. B. & Toutkoushian, R. K. (2006) Overview of economic concepts, models, and methods for institutional research. In Toutkoushian, R. K. & Paulsen, M. B. (Eds) *Applying Economics to Institutional Research.* Hoboken, NJ: Wiley Press.

Price, D. V. & Davis, R. J. (2006) *Institutional Grants and Baccalaureate Degree Attainment.* Washington, DC: National Association of Student Financial Aid Administrators.

Pryor, J. H., Hurtado, S., Deangelo, L., Sharkness, J., Romero, L. C., Korn, W. S. & Tran, S. (2008) *The American Freshman: National Norms for Fall 2008.* Los Angeles: Higher Education Research Institute, UCLA.

Redd, K. E. (2000) *Discounting Toward Disaster: Tuition Discounting, College Finances, and Enrollments of Low-Income Undergraduates.* Indianapolis: USA Group.

Rizzo, M. J. & Ehrenberg, R. G. (2004) Resident and nonresident tuition and enrollment at flagship state universities. In Hoxby, C. M. (Ed.) *College Choices: the Economics of Where To Go, When To Go, and How To Pay For It.* Chicago: University of Chicago Press.

St John, E. P., Asker, E. H. & Hu, S. (2001) The role of finances in student choice: a review of theory and research. In Paulsen, M. B. & Smart, J. C. (Eds) *The Finance of Higher Education: Theory, Research, Policy, and Practice.* New York: Agathon Press.

Steinberg, M. P., Piraino, P. & Haveman, R. (2009) Access to higher education: exploring the variation in Pell grant prevalence among U.S. colleges and universities. *The Review of Higher Education,* 32(2): 235–70.

Toutkoushian, R. K. (2001) Trends in revenues and expenditures for public and private higher education. In Paulsen, M. B. & Smart, J. C. (Eds) *The Finance of Higher Education: Theory, Research, Policy, and Practice.* New York: Agathon Press.

Trow, M. (1984) The analysis of status. In Clark, B. R. (Ed.) *Perspectives on Higher Education: Eight Disciplinary and Comparative Views.* Los Angeles: University of California Press.

Weisbrod, B. A., Ballou, J. P. & Asch, E. D. (2008) *Mission and Money: Understanding the University.* New York: Oxford University Press.

Winston, G. (2004) Differentiation among U.S. colleges and universities. *Review of Industrial Organization,* 24(4): 331–54.

—— (1999) Subsidies, hierarchy and peers: the awkward economics of higher education. *The Journal of Economic Perspectives,* 13(1): 13–36.

Winston, G. C. & Zimmerman, D. J. (2004). Peer effects in higher education. In Hoxby, C. M. (Ed.) *College Choices: the Economics of Where To Go, When To Go, and How To Pay For It.* Chicago: University of Chicago Press.

5

The Developing Student Market in Australian Higher Education

GAVIN MOODIE

In March 1961 the University of Melbourne administered the first *numerus clausus* (closed number) or quota on undergraduate entry in Australia, to the Bachelor of Medicine. This led to the development of a non-monetary "proto market" in higher education, in which the currency is the tertiary entrance rank. Almost 50 years later, on 4 March 2009, the Australian Minister for Education announced the introduction of a "new demand driven funding system" (Gillard, 2009) or public voucher for domestic undergraduate students.

This chapter describes the development and current extent of the marketization of Australian higher education and evaluates its performance against the characteristics of an ideal but feasible market. After a brief overview of the Australian higher education system the chapter describes three successive stages of its marketization: the tertiary entrance rank proto market, tuition fees and income contingent loans, and public vouchers. The chapter concludes by arguing that the Australian domestic student market is limited by geography and discipline. It argues further that any well-designed fees and loans system lacks price signals for students and corresponding price discipline on institutions and that this is a major limitation of any higher education student market.

System Overview

Institutions

Higher education is offered by 40 universities and 65 other higher education providers. Some 37 of the universities are public and have the familiar coinciding gradations of age, status, funding level and research intensity. The public universities dominate higher education provision, enrolling 95 percent of full time equivalent students. There are two small private not-for-profit Australian universities and in 2006 the South Australian government subsidized a private not for profit US university to establish in its capital Adelaide a small presence of 61 full time equivalent students.

Private non-university providers have expanded very fast since 2005 when their students were given access to government guaranteed and subsidized income contingent loans to pay their tuition fees. The private non-university providers are dominated by "for profit" colleges which enrolled 57 percent of private full time equivalent students in 2007. The next biggest group, religious colleges, enrolled 24 percent of private students.

Students

There were 814,700 equivalent full time students enrolled in higher education programs in vocational and higher education institutions in 2007. Some 27 percent of all higher education students are international, one of the highest proportions in the world. The majority 68 percent of students were enrolled in associate and Bachelor degrees, almost all of whom were enrolled in Bachelor degrees. Research higher degree candidates were only 4 percent of total equivalent full time students, which some analysts consider too low to replace the ageing academic workforce and contribute to the nation's research and innovation.

Research

Higher education institutions account for 26 percent of Australia's total expenditure on research and development, but 84 percent of Australia's expenditure on pure basic research. Nonetheless, Australian universities do not conduct mainly pure basic research. Pure basic research is only 27 percent of universities' expenditure on research and development. The other types of research in Australia's classification are strategic basic research which is 22 percent of universities' expenditure, applied research (43 percent) and experimental development (7 percent). By far the biggest field of university research is medical and health sciences, which accounts for 27 percent of universities' expenditure on research and development. Engineering and technology accounts for 11 percent; biological sciences 10 percent; agricultural, veterinary and environmental sciences is 7 percent; and chemical sciences is 5 percent of universities' expenditure on research and development. The rest of universities' expenditure on research and development is spread across 17 fields, each accounting for less than four per cent of expenditure.

Financing

Universities are mainly funded from Australian Government grants which are 41 percent of all universities' funding, and tuition fees from domestic students (23 percent) and international students (15 percent). Australian Government grants are currently allocated to institutions for enrolling the number of full time equivalent students in each disciplinary funding cluster agreed between the government and each institution in annual funding agreements. The

backgrounds transferring from high-cost disciplines to lower cost disciplines (Andrews, 1999: 19).

Third, the introduction of different Hecs bands in 1997 did not reduce the overall demand for law and medicine in the most expensive band and nor did it increase demand for education, humanities, foreign languages and nursing in the least expensive band. Since 2005 the government has allowed public universities to charge domestic students fees up to maxima it determines for each discipline. For some years from 2005 institutions such as the Australian National University, the University of Tasmania and the University of New England charged fees 25 percent lower than other institutions but they did not enjoy an increase in demand. Some institutions such as Macquarie University set their fees at $0 for some science programs, but again the university did not attract additional students in this program from waiving its fees (Moodie, 2009). All institutions have therefore charged the maximum fee permitted since 2008.

Indeed, the whole purpose of income contingent loans is to insulate students from the immediate effect of charging fees and thus to remove the price sensitivity that students might otherwise have. If students were sensitive to fees, the income contingent scheme has been designed poorly and has not met its main reason for existence. But if the income contingent loan scheme has been designed well, as Australia's has, changing fees within a broadly acceptable range will have no effect on student demand. However, the bounds of the broadly acceptable range have yet to be found in Australia (Moodie, 2008).

The marketization of Australian higher education was extended significantly by the Australian government's introduction of income contingent loans for full fee-paying places offered by public and private institutions. In 2002 the government introduced income contingent loans for domestic students enrolled in postgraduate programs, most of which were by then private places funded from full tuition fees, although mostly at public universities. In 2005 the government extended the scheme with some adaptations to undergraduate domestic full fee-paying students enrolled in all approved higher education institutions, public and private. The new Labor Government prohibited public institutions offering private places for domestic students from 2009, but not before some public universities enthusiastically entered the market, and many others participated actively if not as enthusiastically.

It is perhaps subtle, but a distinct effect of the introduction of fees supported by income contingent loans 15 years ago has been the commercialization of public higher education. Notwithstanding Hecs' formal status in its first decade as a government statutory charge, students have always considered it a university fee and expect universities to treat them like paying customers. Students have also become more demanding since they assume that their Hecs charge is the full funding for their place, although initially it was about 20 percent and now it is on average about half the full funding for each student's place. The public also considers even public higher education to be commercial and expects universities to behave accordingly. Partly in reaction to these expectations, university staff have also started to consider even public higher education more commercially. Not all staff consider higher education to be commercial, staff can be inconsistent in considering some aspects of universities commercial and others not, and they can be inconsistent in considering the same activity to be commercial at one level of the organization but not commercial at another level. Nonetheless, there has been a perceptible change in attitudes and behavior in public institutions (Moodie, 2008).

Public Vouchers

From 2012 the Australian government will fund public universities according to their number of full time equivalent undergraduate students in each of nine discipline funding clusters. The Minister of Education insists that she is not introducing vouchers:

> Let me be clear about one important point: this is not a voucher. Students will not be receiving a set dollar entitlement to be redeemed at an institution of their choice. Rather, there will be a Commonwealth payment to universities—with the amount varying depending on the course—on the basis of student numbers.
>
> (Gillard, 2009)

While this is strictly true, the funding arrangement for public institutions will have the same effect as a voucher redeemable at a public institution, and similar arrangements are considered "indirect vouchers" in the literature (see Agasisti et al., 2008: 39 and the literature there cited). However, this will not result in a full competition for domestic undergraduate student places even at public institutions because of constraints of geography and discipline.

Geography and Discipline

Australian undergraduate and postgraduate coursework and research students are not geographically mobile. This is partly a result of undergraduate student income support, which is far more separate from support for tuition fees than in the US and UK. All Australian students are entitled to a government guaranteed and subsidized income contingent loan to pay the fees for any program offered by an approved institution. In contrast, income support is rationed tightly by a means test set very low. While the government has started improving student income support, most students have and will continue to rely on their family and paid work to support themselves while studying. Furthermore, the level of income support is far too low to support any student. Even students on the highest level of income support need paid employment or support from their family to survive. Much of the support students get from their families is in kind such as subsidized board and lodging; it would be less accessible were they to move from the region in which their parents live. So a very high proportion of students commute to university from home, often their parents' home.

Competition in the Australian student market is therefore limited geographically by students' commuting distance. This is not a big limitation in Australian cities with a population of one million or more since they have more than one university, several non-university higher education providers and also some vocational education institutions which also offer higher education programs. However, there is rather less competition in cities and population centers with fewer than one million people. Even an Australian city of 500,000 typically has only one university campus and few if any non-university providers with a very limited range of programs. For people here there is no effective competition for university education, and only very limited competition for higher education. Because of this geographic limit there can be no effective competition in numerous regions and therefore no effective competition for about a third of the higher education student load.

The Australian student market is also limited by discipline. Due to various limitations, even the biggest Australian city can justify only one school of aerospace engineering, agricultural science, dentistry, medical imaging, pharmacy, surveying, veterinary science, most foreign languages and numerous other specializations. So there is no effective competition in these disciplinary specializations.

Evaluation

As a "classical liberal" commentator observed, the conservative Australian Government from 1996 to 2007 was more a "party of private enterprise than free enterprise" (Norton, 2008). It privatized services and constructed markets to increase the role of private bodies rather than to create efficient markets, at times restricting public bodies' participation in the markets it created. In contrast, the Minister for Health and Ageing in the Labor Government from late 2007 expressed the view of many of her colleagues in saying "on the question of public and private, I am agnostic. If it works, I like it" (Roxon, 2008). The 2007 Labor Government thus resumed the policies of the Labor Governments from 1983 to 1996 in seeking to create markets that provide goods and services most efficiently and which most effectively meet the government's social goals. It has explicitly adopted the terminology and to some extent the principles of market or mechanism design for allocating resources (Hurwicz, 1973).

But the domestic student market for higher education is severely limited. In the early chapters of this book Brown demonstrated the gaps and flaws in information available to inform students' decisions as if they were consumers in a higher education market. Some crucial information seems impossible to collect before students make educational choices because it can be obtained only by students' participation in a program, and other information is possible to collect but the practical difficulties make it extremely unlikely that it would be collected or that the cost of collection would outweigh the benefits claimed. Yet other information could readily be collected but is not. Even when relevant information is collected and reported in an accessible form students either ignore or misuse it. Brown argues that for these reasons the student higher education market is at best imperfect since it can never be sufficiently informed to work efficiently. One might add that if students are not informed as consumers of higher education, institutions ipso facto can't be well-informed as providers of higher education since they need well-informed consumers to guide their production.

A further condition for any market is that one good or service may be substituted for another. Yet we saw in the previous section that the Australian higher education student market is limited by geography and discipline. For many disciplines in many regions there is effectively a monopoly and thus no competition in higher education provision. But even for the sizeable disciplines in the sizeable cities the higher education domestic student market is severely restricted if not compromised by its inadequacy of price signals.

Almost all commentators agree that the state must subsidize higher education to avoid what they agree would be an under-investment if institutions had to charge tuition fees to cover all their costs. Most but perhaps not all agree further that the financing mechanism should be designed so that prospective students are not excluded from higher education because they lack the financial means. Human capital theorists argue that human capital is wasted if people are excluded from higher education by any reason other than their ability and incentive to undertake it, and social democrats and others have additional arguments for widening participation in higher education.

So a financing mechanism for higher education is designed well if it protects students from the immediate economic consequences of their decision to study. Yet by its nature such a mechanism also removes any price signal from students and therefore any price discipline on institutions. A good example of such a mechanism and its operation is the Australian income contingent loan scheme described earlier, now implemented in New Zealand (1991), South Africa (1994), Chile (1996), England and Thailand (2006). We noted earlier that with a well-designed income contingent loan scheme, charging students different fees for different disciplines and for studying at different institutions has had no noticeable effect on student demand in general, and in particular, has not affected the demand from students from low socio-economic status backgrounds.

Both Conservative and Labor governments have capped the fees that public institutions may charge under the income contingent loans scheme so it is not possible to test whether student demand is unaffected by whether institutions charge literally all or nothing. But it is clear that at least up to the caps set by government, institutions have no price discipline. Were the government to lift fee caps, at least some institutions would increase their fees without commensurate increases in the quality of their provision, as has been observed in US higher education (Vedder, 2007). The lack of price signals for students and corresponding price discipline on institutions is a major limitation to the higher education student market, and means that at most there can only be a "quasi market" in higher education.

References

Agasisti, T., Cappiello, G. & Catalano, G. (2008) The effects of vouchers in higher education: an Italian case study. *Tertiary Education and Management*, 14(1): 27–42.

Andrews, L. (1999) *Does HECS Deter? Factors Affecting University Participation by Low SES Groups*, Higher Education Division Occasional Paper Series 99-F, Department of Education, Training and Youth Affairs AusInfo, Canberra. http://www.detya.gov.au/archive/highered/occpaper/99F/does.pdf [Accessed on November 11, 1999].

Dill, D. D. (2003) Allowing the market to rule: the case of the United States. *Higher Education Quarterly*, 57(2): 136–57.

Gillard, J. (2009) Introduction Speech. Presented to the *Universities Australia Conference, Canberra*, March 4, 2009. http://www.deewr.gov.au/Ministers/Gillard/Media/Speeches/Pages/Article_090304_155721.aspx [Accessed on March 04, 2009].

Hoxby, C. M. (1997) *The Changing Market Structure of US Higher Education*, Harvard University, mimeo.

Hurwicz, L. (1973) The design of mechanisms for resource allocation. Papers and Proceedings of the 85th Annual Meeting of the American Economic Association. *The American Economic Review*, 63(2): 1–30.

Marginson, S. (2006) Dynamics of national and global competition in higher education. *Higher Education*, 52(1): 1–39.

Moodie, G. (2008) Australia: twenty years of higher education expansion. *Journal of Access, Policy and Practice*, 5(2): 153–79.

—— (2009) Bradley on VET. Paper presented to the *Australian Education Union 2009 National TAFE Council: Annual General Meeting*, Melbourne, January 14.

Norton, A. (2008) More promising signs on vouchers. http://andrewnorton.info/2008/08/more-promising-signs-on-vouchers/#more-541 [Accessed on January 10, 2009].

Queensland Tertiary Admissions Centre (QTAC). (2009) *Year 12 Presentation*, 2009. http://www.qtac.edu.au/Schools/Resources.html [Accessed on March 14, 2009].

Roxon, N. (2008) Private Health under a Labor Government. *Keynote Address to the Australian Private Hospitals Association. 28th National Congress*, Adelaide, October 27. http://www.health.gov.au/internet/ministers/publishing.nsf/Content/sp-yr08-nr-nrsp271008.htm?OpenDocument&yr = 2008&mth = 10 [Accessed on March 31, 2009].

Vedder, R. (2007) *Over Invested and Over Priced: American Higher Education Today*. A Policy Paper from the Center for College Affordability and Productivity, Washington, DC. http://www.collegeaffordability.net/CCAP_Report.pdf [Accessed on November 20, 2007]

6

False Economy? Multiple Markets, Reputational Hierarchy and Incremental Policymaking in UK Higher Education

WILLIAM LOCKE

Introduction

The United Kingdom is often referred to as one of the first countries, after the US, to introduce market conditions in higher education, and to have gone further than most in developing mechanisms to promote market behavior among higher education institutions, students and other consumers of higher education services. This chapter traces the key trends and policies that have given rise to this view and sets them against the conditions for a higher education market set out in Chapter 2. The first section reviews the nature of institutional autonomy, key government policies and the rapid evolution of markets and market behavior in UK higher education. The following two sections review the core markets in students and research. In the third section I argue that a key element of the UK higher education system is a reputational hierarchy of institutions, and explore how university rankings reinforce this hierarchy. The fourth section examines the development of internal markets within institutions, before the concluding section offers a balance sheet. Finally, I suggest that what is missing from a market-based account of higher education may actually undermine its long-term economic efficiency and contribution to society.

Why UK Higher Education was "Market-Ready"

Universities are legally independent from the national governments of England, Scotland, Wales and Northern Ireland—the four constituent nations of the UK. They can employ and dismiss staff, set salaries, decide on academic structure and course content, spend their budgets to achieve their objectives, and own and dispose of their buildings and equipment. Within certain parameters, they can decide on the size of student enrollment and borrow money. In England and Northern Ireland, from 2006, institutions were able to determine the level of tuition fees for full-time undergraduate home and European Union (EU) students up to a maximum "cap". Tuition fees for part-time, postgraduate and international (i.e., non-EU) students are not regulated.

However, despite this organizational autonomy bolstered by increasing levels of private expenditure on higher education, the governments of the UK still exercise a considerable degree of influence over institutions, through the allocation of funding and the conditions attached to this, and the regulation and evaluation of their activities. Intermediary bodies, such as Funding Councils, Research Councils, the Quality Assurance Agency (QAA), the Office of the Independent Adjudicator (OIA) and the Office for Fair Access (OFFA) (in England)—as well as the relevant Government Department or Ministry in each nation—attempt to steer institutions in the direction of government policies, although these policies are not always consistent with each other and can suddenly take a different course (Locke, 2008).

UK higher education institutions (HEIs) are highly differentiated by origin, status, mission, resources, research activity and income, educational provision and student characteristics. The key sub-groupings are fairly stable and largely delineated by age, historical wealth and relative focus on research: the older "research intensive" Russell Group of universities; others that were universities before the abolition of the "binary divide" between polytechnics and universities in 1992; post-1992 universities that had previously been polytechnics; post-2004 universities that were no longer required to possess the power to award research degrees (as distinct from taught degrees) in order to use the title of "university"; and higher education colleges without such powers.

There have been two main waves of expansion in student recruitment over the last 20 years. The first, between 1988 and 1994, saw the number of young students nearly double, as more began to stay on at school, attain entry qualifications and seek higher education. Government and funding council policies facilitated this dramatic growth, as did the expansionism of the post-1992 universities. The second wave, from 2001, was more gradual, as the New Labour Government adopted a policy of expanding participation by 18- to 30-year-olds from the Initial Entry Rate of 41 percent to 50 percent by 2010. This policy eventually hit the rocks of demographic changes and restrictions on government expenditure, now exacerbated by the level of national debt incurred to minimize the effects of the global economic recession on the UK economy. Nevertheless, the demand for higher education shows few signs of abating and, indeed, may grow as labor markets contract and unemployment rises.

Between 1989 and 2003, the public funding of teaching per student in UK higher education declined by 41 percent (Watson and Bowden, 2007); this was much sharper—although from a higher starting point—than in most other countries (Mayhew et al., 2004). Total spending on tertiary education is now 1.3 percent of GDP, including public spending of 0.9 percent, one of the lowest levels of any OECD country (OECD, 2008). Some institutions have been running accumulated deficits and many are operating surpluses well below the recommended limit (HEFCE, 2006). Partly as a consequence, mergers of smaller and specialist institutions with larger universities mean there are fewer HEIs now (169) than in 1994/95 (186) (UUK, 2008). Economic recession, the English Government's decision to limit the growth of UK and other EU student numbers, and substantial recent reductions in public expenditure on higher education could result in the first British university going bankrupt, being broken up and the more viable parts sold off to private companies (Fazackerley, 2009).

Recruiting the Right Students

By the 1980s, British higher education had most of the attributes of a market system, but it was not until the sudden cuts in public expenditure at the beginning of that decade that universities began to behave in a market-orientated fashion (Williams, 2004). Faced with the financial stringency of the new Conservative government, most went about finding new sources of income, including recruiting students from outside the EU from whom they were now required to demand fees covering the full costs of provision but, crucially, also allowed to charge more. Financial memoranda—or contracts between the funding councils and individual institutions—were put in place. These set prices for each student recruited to one of four categories—or bands—of subject depending on differences in cost, determined by the level of laboratory or other facilities provision. The memoranda also established the conditions for the money allocated, in effect securing what has since become a highly regulated market in higher education.

One further significant change was made in the 1980s: the transfer of approximately 20 percent of the funding grant for teaching to subsidize the payment of fees by individual students direct to their institution. This helped to fuel the first of the recent waves of expansion. The rapid expansion of higher education in the early 1990s prompted a debate about whether students or graduates should bear some of the costs of their higher education, given that they would enjoy considerable personal (i.e., private) benefit from it.

However, the introduction of upfront tuition fees of £1,100 per year from 1998 was not popular among the British electorate. As the Westminster government began to devolve some of its powers, including education policy, to the smaller nations, Scotland replaced the fees with a graduate contribution scheme and has subsequently abolished payment by Scottish-domiciled students for full-time undergraduate education altogether. The income from the new fees was also insufficient to plug the £10bn funding gap that had opened up (UUK, 2002) during the steady decline in the unit of resource since the 1980s. From 2006, the new regime—in which UK and other EU students could take out interest subsidized loans equivalent to the tuition fee and make income-contingent repayments after graduation—was intended to introduce a market in fees, with institutions varying the level according to the popularity and costs of their courses and, theoretically, the likely benefits to be enjoyed by the graduates of

accompanied by a further regulatory instrument: with competition for research funds came the RAE; with independence for polytechnics from local authority control came financial memoranda; with expansion of student numbers came Teaching Quality Assessment (TQA) and, eventually, the QAA; with the introduction of upfront tuition fees came pressure from government to widen participation to previously underrepresented social groups; with the relaxation of the conditions for university title in England and Wales came the principle of renewable powers to award taught degrees (albeit only for privately funded organizations); and with increased but deferred tuition fees (again in England) came OFFA.

Quality

The combination of government regulation and institutional (and not just academic) self-regulation has aimed to ensure a minimum threshold in teaching, and selectivity in research. But it is status and the reputational hierarchy of institutions that is valued more by many students and their families, graduate employers and the media. Various initiatives have sought to standardize higher education provision in the UK, but it has been the imitation of the "elite" universities by those who aspire to climb the rankings that has led to increasing isomorphism in the sector. Indeed, an earlier concern with quality *processes* (in TQA and Quality Audit) appears to have been replaced by a preoccupation with *outcomes*, particularly the contribution of higher education to the economy and, increasingly, its role in business survival and economic recovery.

So, the bottom line for UK HE plc seems to indicate the gradual privatization of a mass higher education system which, nevertheless, continues to be dominated by an enduring reputational hierarchy of institutions. Those universities and colleges with sufficient resources and expertise have responded to incremental changes in government policies with entrepreneurial zeal, but their market behavior is still highly regulated in the key areas of price, numbers and market entry. Consumers, on the other hand, are hampered by limited information about the value added by specific education and research provision which is all too often obscured by reputation and status. What is missing from this account are the non-market benefits of higher education.

Valuing the Non-Market Benefits of Higher Education

McMahon (2009) asks whether the current trend toward privatization within universities and colleges should continue, and if so, how far it should go. He acknowledges that some privatization generates more resources for institutions, but argues that too much can result in economic inefficiency and threaten the social benefits of higher education that we have come to take for granted and, perhaps, begun to undervalue. These wider benefits include the training of a highly skilled workforce, but also a greater propensity among graduates for life-long learning, better health, civic participation, intercultural understanding and environmental awareness and a lower likelihood of unemployment, criminal activity and poor health. The evidence for higher education's contribution to more deep-seated transformations, such as social mobility and equity, is perhaps less convincing, at least until there is universal higher education in the UK and the reputational hierarchy of institutions has been replaced by genuine parity of esteem and real diversity.

For our purposes, however, McMahon's key argument is that, if the social and private non-market benefits of higher education become undervalued or are even ignored, politicians and the electorate are unlikely to want to maintain the proportion of the public contribution to higher education in relation to the private investment of students, businesses and others willing to pay for its services, even as the latter increases. This, I want to argue, would be a false economy. It would divert universities and colleges toward meeting private needs and away from their wider, social purposes. If institutions cannot recoup the costs of providing wider benefits, the risk is that these will be undersupplied. The ultimate losers will be society and broader and longer term economic efficiency. Moreover, if institutions are simply seen to be maximizing revenues, they risk losing consumers'—and, ultimately, the public's—trust. An example of this from the UK is the aggressive recruitment of international students and inadequate provision to meet their educational and social needs once they have arrived on campus. This is a case where institutional self-interest can put at risk the collective interest of the sector. A good reputation may be hard won over many decades or, for a few universities, many centuries, but—as we have recently seen among retailers, banks and even democratic institutions in the UK—it can be quickly lost.

References

Adams, J. & Bekhradnia, B. (2004) *What Future for Dual Support?* Oxford: Higher Education Policy Institute.

Fazackerley, A. (2009) *Sink or Swim? Facing up to Failing Universities.* London: Policy Exchange.

Higher Education Funding Council for England (HEFCE). (2006) *Financial Forecasts and Annual Monitoring Statements: Outcomes for 2005,* Circular 2006/01, January, Bristol: Higher Education Funding Council for England.

Johnson, H. (2003) The marketing orientation in higher education: the perspectives of academics about its impact on their role. In Williams, G. (Ed.) *The Enterprising University: Reform, Excellence and Equity,* Buckingham: Open University Press/Society for Research into Higher Education.

Leathwood, C. (2004) A critique of institutional inequalities in higher education or an alternative to hypocrisy in higher educational policy, *Theory and Research in Education,* 2(1): 31–48.

—— (2008) Institutional stratification and higher education policy: choice, diversity and social justice, paper to *the Society for Research in Higher Education Policy Network,* June 30.

Locke, W. (2004) Integrating research and teaching strategies: implications for institutional management and leadership in the United Kingdom, *Higher Education Management and Policy,* 16(1): 101–20.

—— (2008) Higher education policy in England: missed opportunities, unintended consequences and unfinished business, *Journal of Access Policy and Practice*, 5(2): 181–208.

Locke, W. & Bótas, P. C. P. (2009) The academic labour market in the United Kingdom: fully developed or quasi-market? Paper presented to *The 22nd Consortium of Higher Education Researchers (CHER) Annual Conference*, Porto, Portugal, September 10–12, 2009.

Locke, W., Verbik, L., Richardson, J. & King, R. (2008) *Counting What Is Measured or Measuring What Counts? League Tables and Their Impact on Higher Education Institutions in England*, Bristol: Education Funding Council for England (HEFCE).

Mayhew, K., Deer, C. & Dua, M. (2004) The move to mass higher education in the UK: many questions and some answers, *Oxford Review of Education*, 30(1): 65–82.

McMahon, W. (2009) *Higher Education, Greater Good: The Private and Social Benefits of Higher Education*, Baltimore, MD: The Johns Hopkins University Press.

Organisation for Economic Co-operation and Development (OECD). (2008) *Education at a Glance: OECD Indicators 2008*, Paris: Organisation for Economic Co-operation and Development, http://www.SourceOECD.org.

Powell, S. & Green, H. (2006) The national funding of doctoral training: Warnings from the English experience, *Journal of Higher Education Policy and Management*, 28(3): 263–75.

Universities UK (UUK). (2002) *Investing for Success*, Spending Review Submission, London: Universities UK.

—— (2003) *Funding Research Diversity*, London: Universities UK.

—— (2006) *Monitoring Research Diversity: Changes between 2000 and 2005*, London: Universities UK.

—— (2007) *HE in Facts and Figures: Research and Innovation*, London: Universities UK.

—— (2008) *Patterns of Higher Education Institutions in the UK: Eighth Report*, London: Universities UK.

—— (2009) *Monitoring Research Concentration and Diversity: Changes between 1994 and 2007*, London: Universities UK.

Watson, D. (2008) Universities behaving badly? *Higher Education Review*, 40(3): 3–14.

Watson, D. & Bowden, R. (2007) The fate of the Dearing recommendations: policy and performance in UK HE, 1997–2007. In Watson, D. & Amoah, M. (Eds) *The Dearing Report: Ten Years On*, Bedford Way Papers, London: Institute of Education, University of London.

Williams, G. (2004) The higher education market in the United Kingdom. In Teixeira, P. N., Jongbloed, B., Dill, D. D. & Amaral, A. (Eds) *Markets in Higher Education: Rhetoric or Reality?* Dordrecht: Kluwer Academic Publishers.

Zemsky, R. (2005) The dog that doesn't bark: why markets neither limit prices n or promote educational quality. In Burke, J. & Associates (Eds) *Achieving Accountability in Higher Education: Balancing Public, Academic and Market Demands*. San Francisco: Jossey-Bass.

7

Markets in Dutch Higher Education
Improving Performance and Quality in a Hands-Off Governance Setting

BEN JONGBLOED

Introduction

The higher education system in the Netherlands is increasingly characterized by market elements. Ever since the late 1980s, producer and consumer sovereignty increased steadily. Today, Dutch higher education providers operate relatively independently from the government, and by positioning themselves strategically in the market try to gain a competitive advantage over other providers and generate revenues from various activities. Students have a large freedom to choose. They pay tuition fees, and have seen their student grants becoming increasingly tied to study performance criteria. This chapter will try to illustrate this by presenting a large number of facts and trends on the Dutch higher education system.

Dutch higher education is organized as a binary system. *Research universities* focus on the independent practice of research-oriented work in an academic or professional setting. They train students in academic study and research, although many study programs also have a professional component. *Universities of Applied Sciences* (UAS; in Dutch: *hogescholen*) are more practically oriented, preparing students directly for specific careers. Their study programs focus on the practical application of knowledge. There are 14 research universities and 41 UAS. The UAS award mostly Bachelor's degrees. Only some award Master's degrees. In terms of student numbers, the UAS are the biggest sector (370,000 BA and 12,000 MA students in 2008). The research universities enroll 219,000 students (146,000 BA and 73,000 MA). Total expenditures on higher education institutions equal the EU19 average (1.3 percent of GDP). Most of the expenditures (1 percent of GDP) originate from the public sector; 0.3 percent is from the private sector. In a strictly legal sense, almost all UAS and three research universities are private institutions. However, all receive public funds on the same terms and are held to the same regulations. There are also some privately funded universities and institutions of higher professional education.

The Netherlands is a front-runner as far as the Bologna Process is concerned. The three-tier system was fully implemented in 2002. The average university Bachelor's program leading to a Bachelor of Arts (BA) or Bachelor of Science (BSc) degree takes three years and provides a broad but predominantly in-depth basis for further specialization. In *hogescholen*, the BA degree lasts four years due to the fact that compared to the research universities the students have had a shorter secondary education. A recent (2006) innovation is the two-year associate degree in the UAS. University Master of Arts (MA) or Master of Science (MSc) degree courses take one to two years to complete, depending on the discipline. PhD degree courses leading to the title of Doctor are only available from research universities and entail four years of full-time research under the supervision of a professor.

Governance

The Ministry of Education, Culture and Science has overall responsibility for the governance of the public higher education institutions and the public research organizations in the system. Unlike the UK, there is no intermediary funding council, although there is a research council allocating competitive funding to research universities. The bulk of the recurrent public funding derives directly from the education ministry.

In 1985 the white paper "Higher Education: Autonomy and Quality" (HOAK) was released. It set in motion a movement away from an "interventionary state" toward a more "facilitatory state" in higher education (Neave and Van Vught, 1991). The 1993 *Higher Education and Research Act* codified the enhanced institutional autonomy and introduced the principle of self-regulation for higher education institutions. Since then, the policy framework revolves mostly around funding and quality assurance. The HOAK paper introduced *quality assurance* as a policy instrument in the steering philosophy. In exchange for more autonomy, the higher education institutions were expected to play an active role in the establishment of a new quality assurance system for teaching and research. In disciplines with an explicit vocational character the world of work was to be represented. Quality assurance was based on self-evaluation reports prepared by the institutions and site visits were carried out by experts (peers) in the field for each disciplinary area in a six-year cycle. The system is believed to function well and still is in place today, although some changes were made over time such as the introduction of accreditation in 2004. The acceptance of the system is also due to the fact that government does not translate the outcomes of the quality assessments into its budget allocations.

In the ruling coalition government's policy program one of the main policy objectives is to create an innovative, competitive and entrepreneurial economy. The main challenges are identified in the *Strategic Agenda for higher education, research and science* (November 2007) of the Education ministry. The starting point is that the current position of the Dutch economy and the Dutch research system is good, but fragile. Research policy will need to contribute to raising labor productivity by strengthening the link between education and knowledge institutions, on the one hand, and businesses, societal and governmental organizations, on the other.

A related challenge is to stimulate top-level research and to create an ambitious learning and research culture. Not only should the quality of education and research be improved, but the quantity of well-trained knowledge workers is a main challenge. Shortages are looming, especially in the fields of science and technology. While the ruling Cabinet embraced the Lisbon objectives and recognizes that education and research are vital for the Dutch knowledge society and the knowledge economy, it has so far found it hard to realize the objective of spending 3 percent of GDP on R&D.

Funding

Over time, the higher education institutions saw the share of third-party funds in their revenues increase as they became more entrepreneurial and government funding declined. In 2007, the share reached 14 percent in the UAS sector and 28 percent in universities. Tuition fee income represents 6 percent in universities and 18 for UAS. The government sets the level of tuition fees in the publicly funded institutions for full-time students. Fees have increased gradually and are about 1,600 Euros for all EU students, irrespective of program or institution. Part-time students and students from non-EU countries pay a rate that is set by the institution. The Dutch universities were keen to provide courses given in English. Nowadays more than half of all the Master's degrees on offer are entirely in English and about 12 percent of all students at research universities are international students.

The government operational grant to higher education institutions is predominantly formula-based and provided as a block grant. Each research university receives a lump sum for teaching and research. UAS receive no research budget as such, but from the year 2001 onward the UAS received an additional budget for "*lectors*". Lectors are similar to an associate professor in research universities. They carry out applied research that directly benefits the teaching in their discipline and they engage in two-way knowledge transfer with (regional) businesses. For the research universities, the research component in the lump sum is relatively large (58 percent) and performance-driven in the sense that more than one-third is based on diplomas (BA, MA and PhD) and allocations for accredited Research Schools. This part of the recurrent operational grant allows universities to carry out fundamental, curiosity-driven research.

The ruling Cabinet now has developed plans to introduce a funding model that will rely less on diplomas and mostly on numbers of enrolled students. In order to keep the institutions focussed on getting students to a degree, institutions will only receive funding for students that have not yet exceeded the normative time to degree (three or four years for a Bachelor, one or two for a Master's degree). The model will award 80 percent of the teaching funds on the basis of the numbers of enrolled students and BA and MA diplomas. The amount per student in the different cost bands will be the same as the amount per diploma. The model will apply to research universities as well as to UAS. The new formula will distribute 20 percent of the funding in the form of institution-specific budgets, to be based partly on quality of teaching and partly on additional policy objectives. However, the introduction of the model is postponed until 2011. In recent years we observe a tendency to set part of the block grant aside in contracts where institutions agree with the Ministry of Education to work on specific objectives like improving access for socially disadvantaged groups, or increasing the quality of teaching.

Institutions' third-party funds consist of a heterogeneous mix of revenues from activities such as contract research (approximately half of the third stream), contract teaching, consultancies, research commercialization, endowments and renting out university facilities. Clients are private businesses, government, non-profit organizations and the European Union. Where most third-party funds are driven by external demands, the research projects funded by the Research Council are overwhelmingly for fundamental research and very competitive.

In recent years the UAS also have been encouraged to generate third-party funding. Apart from the funds for lectors (see earlier) we mention the RAAK subsidy scheme. The RAAK-program (*Regional Attention and Action for Knowledge Circulation*) aims to stimulate regional research collaboration between UAS and business (in particular small- and medium-sized enterprises) with a view to developing joint innovation activities and stimulating knowledge exchange. All of this is also very much in line with the ambition of UAS to become fully fledged knowledge institutions that play an important role in their region. One has to remember that until the middle of the 1980s the UAS were still not regarded as part of the higher education system. After large scale mergers and amalgamations that reduced their number from over 430 to about 40, the UAS have become mature and well-developed institutions that serve the largest share of students in higher education. Many of the UAS students are from families that 20 years ago would not have sent their children to university. On top of that, employers have shown appreciation for UAS graduates.

Students

According to CBS (2008), the UAS enrolled 270,600 students in 1995/96 and 374,400 in 2007/08. In this period the percentage of full-time students declined from 84 in 1995/96 to 81 in 2007/08. The percentage of part-time students increased from 15 in 1995/96 to 16 in 2007/08. Research universities enrolled

Table 7.1 Percentage of 2002/03 student cohort that have obtained a degree

	After 3 years	After 4 years	After 5 years	After 6 years
Research university	22	42	59	69
UAS	11	42	57	64

Source: CBS Statline.

177,700 students in 1995/96 and 212,700 in 2007/08. In this period their percentage of full- and part-time students kept at the same level. Two interesting trends stand out in this period. First, female students now hold the majority in UAS as their percentage increased from 49 in 1995/96 to 52 in 2007/08; in research universities their percentage increased from 46 to 51. Second, the share of non-Dutch students (actually, students that have at least one parent with a non-Dutch nationality) has increased rapidly in the period 1995–2007 to about a quarter of all students.

Table 7.1 provides some facts about study progress, illustrating that after five years almost 60 percent has earned a degree. Please note that the stipulated time for a BA degree is three years in research universities and four years in the UAS sector. The relatively long time to degree is caused by the fact that Dutch higher education is characterized by open access, meaning that institutions have to accept all students that meet the minimum entrance requirements. In other words, there is no selection. When the number of applicants exceeds the national teaching capacity or (in very exceptional cases) the needs of the labor market, the education minister decides upon the number of places (nationally and at the institutional level) which will be available. This is known as a *numerus fixus*. Students are then selected through a so-called weighted-lottery system. This provides higher chances for candidates with higher average examination results in secondary education. Since September 2000 higher education institutions have been given more autonomy in determining their teaching capacity. They can allocate a maximum of 10 percent of the total available places on the basis of student motivation, working experience or talent.

In recent years, the institutions have become more concerned about drop-out rates and have introduced initiatives to increase retention and refer underperforming students or students that feel they made the wrong choice of program to alternative programs. In some cases, universities have introduced performance criteria. In the Master's phase the universities are allowed to offer more selective (and specially accredited) *Research Master's* programs that are targeted in particular at students that wish to pursue a research-oriented career and/or continue to a PhD. In the Bachelor's phase such selective programs aimed at excellent students are offered by a few universities (Utrecht, Maastricht, Amsterdam) in the shape of *university colleges* and *honors tracks*.

Most BA students, in particular those going to a UAS, choose an institution in their region, partly because there is a good spread of UAS institutions of equal quality across the country and partly because many UAS students choose to live with their parents. The research universities have a slightly larger catchment area. For their Master's, most research universities recruit their students from the Netherlands as a whole.

Subjects Offered

In terms of degree programs, the research universities offered 444 Bachelor programs and 893 Master programs in 2007. The UAS offered 207 Bachelor programs and 66 Master programs in 2008. These figures only refer to the individual programs that are included in the official register of accredited programs. From the year 2006 onward, the UAS sector also offers short (two-year) Associate Degree programs. There are about 40, provided on an experimental basis. Unlike research universities, the UAS in principle do not receive government funding for the Master's programs they offer. However, the government has made a few exceptions to this rule and does fund some MA programs for selected professions in teacher training, fine arts, health and social work.

The research university sector offers the largest variety in programs, in particular at Master's level. In many research universities the number of students in Master's programs is relatively small and this has an impact on the cost per student. The Research Master programs in universities are even more costly as these are selective two-year programs targeted at students aiming to pursue a research career.

The degree of competition for students depends very much on the disciplinary area. For instance, in the economics cluster the combined market shares of the four largest research universities lies close to 70 percent, which is an indication of a relatively concentrated market with oligopolistic tendencies. In the UAS sector, this concentration index is almost 40 percent, indicating a more competitive market. The latter is also the case for the social sciences cluster in the UAS. For the social sciences, the degree of competition among research universities is again much less high.

The scale of the programs and the degree of competition are two factors determining the cost per student. However, the most important driver of program cost is the disciplinary area the program belongs to. Classroom-based programs obviously are less expensive than laboratory-based programs and ones in the health-related subjects. The allocation model used for the public funding takes such factors into account, but only to some extent. Public funding per student in current prices declined from 5,500 Euros per student in 1996 to 4,900 in 2006. In the same period the tuition fee increased from 1,090 to 1,520 Euros. Given the fact that research universities spend on average some 8,000 Euros per student, the tuition fee is about 20 percent of student costs. Because the direct public contribution represents about two-thirds, this implies that universities are cross-subsidizing their teaching using revenues from other sources of income, in particular from research. This is the case in particular for degree programs in the natural sciences and medicine (Jongbloed et al., 2004).

Autonomy

In the Netherlands a substantial number of market conditions are present already (Jongbloed, 2003). From the late 1980s onward many powers were devolved from the government to the higher education institutions. In the middle of the 1990s the UAS (in 1994) and the research universities (in 1995), became the owner of their buildings, receiving an increase in their operational grant to support their infrastructure. At the end of the 1990s, control over the terms of employment was almost fully decentralized from the ministry to the higher education institutions. Institutions are nowadays free to appoint regular full-time senior academic staff, to determine the salaries of their staff, to borrow funds on the capital market, to build up reserves and/or carry over unspent financial resources from one year to the next. Much earlier they had been granted freedom to determine how they spend their public operational grant and to generate most categories of private funding. Institutions are also relatively free to specify the contents of their programs and curricula. As regards the issue of transparency and program choice, one sees more and more information about providers and programs becoming available through websites, study guides and open days. For students, choice of program remains problematic because of the large numbers of programs on offer with some institutions allowing students some room to choose specific program specializations, support facilities and individualized options in combining learning, working and caring for a family. The wide choice range, combined with the open entry character of Dutch higher education, is one of the reasons for the relatively high drop out rates.

The government still has a large say in the approval of new degree programs. Providers can introduce new programs only after initial accreditation by the accreditation agency. The ministry checks, after advice by a special commission, whether a new program duplicates an already existing one. If so, it may decide to withhold funding on the basis of *macro-efficiency* considerations. For new providers, barriers to entry exist because government funding is available only to a limited number of "officially recognized" providers. Recognition implies that new entrants have to meet general criteria in terms of administration, governance, staffing and facilities. Newcomers also have to undergo a program quality check. Full-time students in recognized institutions qualify for student support, but the institutions themselves do not automatically receive public funding, unless they are added to the list of publicly funded institutions mentioned in the law.

The hands-off type of government steering has opened the door for more pronounced competition. Universities and UAS are triggered to establish distinct profiles and explicit strategic planning has become common. Higher education institutions are stimulated to create their own niches and have intensified their efforts to generate "private funding" and income from project funding. Both in teaching and in research, such third-party funding has grown rapidly since the mid-1980s. Nowadays, no single Dutch higher education institution would survive without this source of income. The increased competition so far has not led to any excessive promotional activities by institutions. Attracting students or generating third-party funds takes place less on the basis of marketing campaigns and mostly on the institutions' reputation in delivering quality and value for money.

The shift toward self-regulation in the sector has had large implications for central institutional management. In earlier days institutional management was relatively weak but nowadays it has gained in importance. In 1997, the Dutch parliament passed the *Modernising University Governance Structures* bill, which marked the end of an era of participatory modes of internal university governance. Executive leadership (rectors and deans) was strengthened and representative bodies where academics, non-academics and students held seats became advisory rather than decision-making bodies. Each institution installed a supervisory board (a Board of Trustees), consisting of external members. The board acts as a buffer between the government and the institution's executives.

Research Funds and Research Policy

Before we discuss academic research we present some basic facts on R&D—its level and where it is performed (Table 7.2).

The Netherlands spends less than the average for the EU-27 countries, which is 1.84 percent of GDP. It falls well short of the 3 percent Lisbon target. The public part of the Dutch research landscape consists of research universities and UAS institutions—together HERD in Table 7.2—and the government labs (GOVERD), such as the institutes owned by the Research Council or Academy of Sciences and the laboratories operated by the Netherlands Organization for Applied Research (TNO). The research universities perform most of the public R&D as the UAS sector is still a relative newcomer.

The research policy framework revolves very much around funding and quality assurance mechanisms that stress excellence and relevance. In recent years, a

Table 7.2 Dutch R&D expenditures by sector of performance, as a percentage of GDP (2006)

Higher education (HERD)	Private sector (BERD)	Government research institutes (GOVERD)	Total (GERD)
0.47%	0.96%	0.24%	1.67%

Source: Eurostat.

large emphasis was placed on policies to encourage the transfer of knowledge from academia to industry, in particular through the promotion of public–private partnerships and the creation of spin-off companies. Please note that outcomes of academic research are owned by the university.

The funding that research universities receive for R&D is to be understood in the context of their overall funding framework, described earlier. If we combine the various components of the universities' recurrent funds that are performance-driven (about €650m in 2007), add the Research Council funds (about €300m) and the contract research income (about €600m), one may conclude that, at present, some two-thirds of the universities' research revenues is based on performance. The funding of university research has become more performance-driven and certainly more competitive in recent decades. Research Council funding and contract funding have increased. Slightly over half of all university researchers these days are paid through competitive grants. More staff, therefore, are on short-term contracts. The absolute number of researchers funded through recurrent funding has nevertheless remained largely stable.

Accountability in research activities is ensured through *research assessments*. All universities adhere to a uniform evaluation procedure, the *Standard Evaluation Protocol for Public Research Organizations* (SEP), developed jointly by the universities, the Academy of Sciences and the Research Council. The assessments take place every six years. Evaluators (*peers*) rate the quality of research programs in terms of four criteria: academic quality; scientific productivity; scientific relevance; scientific long-term viability.

The ratings make use of a five-point scale, where a rating of five represents excellent research and a rating of one indicates poor research. Out of the 146 research groups assessed in the period 2003–05, more than 40 percent received a rating indicating very good research, while almost 30 percent scored "excellent". The overall quality of academic research in most university research programs therefore is good to very good, a judgment confirmed by international comparisons.

The quality assessment protocol requires universities also to evaluate the training of doctoral students—the so-called AiOs (in Dutch: *Assistent in Opleiding*). An AiO is a doctoral candidate who obtains a four-year appointment in the university as an "assistant in training" and actually earns a salary. It is a distinct academic position, at the bottom of the ladder that leads from lecturer, assistant professor, associate professor to full professor. An AiO receives advanced research training by way of active participation in research and, to a limited extent (less than 25 percent of working time), in teaching and administration. Research training is a very hot topic, given the imminent retirement wave of professors. By carefully organizing and structuring research groups, universities nowadays try to create the required financial room to appoint new (young) professors. The *tenure track* system is on the rise, supported by monitoring systems that keep an eye on the quantitative and qualitative research performance of research staff.

The Research Council is an important mechanism for the training and retention of researchers. The *Innovational Research Incentives Scheme* provides individualized research grants. It consists of three different personal subsidy forms, each of which is oriented at a specific phase in the scientific career: young PhD holders; experienced researchers; and researchers on the verge of a professorship. The government has recently decided to extend this scheme with €50m annually for the coming years.

Policies

With respect to research policy developments one needs to pay attention to science and innovation policy, as this heavily determines today's institutions' strategies and resourcing. The main aims of research policy of the Education Ministry, as stated in its recent Science Budget, are:

1. increasing focus and concentration;
2. promoting the utilization of research results;
3. training and retaining researchers and other knowledge workers;
4. promoting top-quality research by encouraging competition.

To create focus and concentration (i.e., critical mass), three national themes—Information & Communication Technology (ICT), genomics/life sciences, nanotechnology—have been selected. In addition, the Research Council has developed 13 multidisciplinary themes, for which thematic programs were developed. Individual researchers then submit proposals for undertaking research, often in teams, some of them incorporating private partners. Performance-related funding for university research also contributes to the emergence of research concentrations. It is believed that academic research capacity is still very much scattered, reducing its impact.

To promote the utilization of research results, the research policy is aimed at expanding current strengths in the Dutch knowledge system. Excellent R&D partnerships are given more leeway (networks, consortia, "hotspots"). Utilization is also promoted by several programs that provide grants to public–private research consortia using the tax proceeds from natural gas exploitation.

As regards training and retention, the government holds institutions responsible for their personnel policy. The "established posts" principle is gradually being replaced by a career principle to strengthen the training and retaining of researchers and other knowledge workers.

The objective of promoting top-quality research is mainly realized by encouraging competition. This takes place through performance-based funding for university research, the Research Council policies, and the incentives for research co-operation with business enterprises.

There are several overlaps between research policy and the Economic Affairs ministry's innovation policy, including the promotion of spin-offs from universities, strengthening the link between universities and small and medium-sized enterprises, stimulating co-operation between industry and the public research infrastructure, and increasing the participation of Dutch industry in public (applied and fundamental) research, especially in key areas.

The *Leading Technology Institutes* (LTIs) are public–private research partnerships created to encourage public–private collaboration and innovation in areas that have a strong counterpart in Dutch industry. There are nine LTIs receiving start-up funding from government and industry for a period of 10 years. Universities and (semi-) public research institutes participate in the LTIs. The first four LTIs started in the late 1990s and the 2002 evaluation suggested that the LTI model was successful and should be continued. Five other LTIs were initiated and three non-technical Societal Top Institutes were added recently, covering the fields of pensions/ageing, urban innovation and international law.

Conclusion

Two things stand out when one observes the developments in the Dutch higher education sector in recent decades. The first is the increased attention paid over the years to strengthening autonomy and quality. Emphasizing autonomy and quality began in the 1980s, but in the 1990s it changed gear and started to also emphasize the economic impact and relevance of institutions' activities. Related to the latter is the emergence of a "third task" for institutions in addition to their traditional task of providing degree programs and carrying out scientific research. In short, *quality and performance* have become the key goals in Dutch higher education, although the meaning of the two concepts nowadays is slightly different compared to 25 years ago.

It can also be seen that "hands-off" governance mechanisms are gradually being replaced by a different approach. Where the government realizes it can no longer play a central role and plan higher education and research from the top, it tries to promote universities becoming more connected to organizations from outside the traditional academic circles. Such networks exert an important influence on the governance and functioning. Within this network approach, policy-makers try to support specific areas of research (and economic) potential such as life sciences/genomics, nanotechnology and social innovation. In a way the consensus-based governance model—the "polder model"—that the Netherlands is known for still prevails, because the choice of instruments, the areas of strategic interest and the building of networks require a great deal of stakeholder involvement. However, the various actors operate much more in a market-like setting stressing performance and value for money.

References

Centraal Bureau Voor De Statistiek (CBS) (2008) *Jaarboek Onderwijs 2009*. Den Haag: Centraal Bureau voor de Statistiek (CBS). Den Haag/Heerlen.

Jongbloed, B. (2003) Marketisation in Higher Education, Clark's Triangle and the essential ingredients of markets. *Higher Education Quarterly*, 57(2): 110–35.

Jongbloed, B., Salerno, C. & Kaiser, F. (2004) *Kosten per Student: Methodologie, Schattingen en een Internationale Vergelijking*. (Translation: Cost per Student). The Hague: DeltaHage/Ministry of Education.

Neave, G. & Van Vught, F. (1991) *Prometheus Bound: The Changing Relationship Between Government and Higher Education in Western Europe*. Oxford: Pergamon Press.

8

Portuguese Higher Education
More Competition and Less Market Regulation?

PEDRO TEIXEIRA AND ALBERTO AMARAL

Introduction

In this chapter we analyze some major trends in the marketization of Portuguese higher education. First, we will present the main factors that seem to have strengthened competition. In the following two sections we discuss to what extent this trend has represented a move towards greater marketization (Wolf Jr, 1993; Le Grand and Bartlett, 1993), namely by referring to the implications in Portugal of some current important European trends in higher education policy, such as the Bologna process and the move towards accreditation. We will finish with some concluding remarks on the implications and coherence of these complex trends.

Competition in Portuguese Higher Education

Competitive Forces on the Supply Side—Spatial and Disciplinary Concentration

Competition has been stimulated by certain major features of higher education supply in Portugal. Some of these have to do with the way the system has developed into mass higher education and especially the types of institutional strategies adopted (and the way the system was regulated) (Teixeira et al., 2004). However, the recent financial context has also stimulated further competition between institutions.

One of the most important changes has been in regional concentration (Nunes, 2000). One of the leading elements of several major reforms, since the early 1970s, has been the expansion of the higher education network, in order to speed up the country's economic modernization, by changing its pattern of uneven geographical distribution (Teixeira et al., 2006). It was expected that this expansion would be an engine of growth in the less developed regions, by improving the qualifications of the labor force and providing an important stimulus for economic activity. Thus, reforms in the 1970s and 1980s created new public universities and university institutes in several medium-sized cities across the country, as well as public polytechnic institutes and teacher training

Table 8.1 Distribution of enrollments by region (%)

Region	1967	1991	2001			2007			Population
			Public	Private	Total	Public	Private	Total	15–24 years
North	18.5	26.8	27.5	37.1	30.3	27.5	41.7	31.0	38
Centre	24.6	18.0	26.3	8.3	21.0	26.3	7.1	21.5	21
Lisbon	56.9	49.6	33.2	51.4	38.5	34.6	48.1	38.0	24
South	—	4.2	10.8	2.8	8.5	9.4	2.6	7.7	11
Islands	—	1.4	2.2	0.4	1.7	2.2	0.5	1.8	6
Total	100.0	100.0	100.0	100.0	100.0	100.0	100.0	100.0	100

Source: Nunes (2000); INE (2008); GPEARI (2008).

schools. The early 1980s witnessed a growing geographical diversification of the public higher education system. Higher education reached all regions, breaking with a secular pattern of strong spatial concentration (see Table 8.1).

The development of the vocational sector was followed by the rapid growth of the private sector, which did not contribute much to regional diversification (Amaral and Teixeira, 2000). Contrary to the expectations of many observers, private institutions invested in the main urban areas of Lisbon and Porto, almost ignoring other important urban areas in the central region. Hence the regional distribution of the higher education network became much more concentrated.

Despite the diversification attempts, Portuguese higher education continued to reproduce the distribution pattern of the population and economic activities, matching the regional concentrations and disparities. The highest numbers of institutions, as well as the largest (and also those with more prestige and scientific recognition), are located in the two metropolitan areas of Lisbon and Porto (Simão et al., 2002). Second-tier cities remain with the universities or polytechnic institutes of smaller size and doubtful sustainability in some courses or programs, depending on their education component more than on their research activities to survive. Overall, the system presents a significant trend toward spatial concentration, which creates significant competition between institutions.

This strong spatial concentration was reinforced by programmatic concentration, again promoted by actions of the private sector (Teixeira and Amaral, 2007). During the period of rapid growth, private institutions concentrated on low-cost popular programs, namely social sciences (law, business, management), which rapidly became saturated. The presence of the private sector in more technical and costlier areas was significantly lower than in the public sector, with the exception of health sciences (see Table 8.2). In this case, in recent years there was an emerging divide between the university and polytechnic branches of the private sector, because although private universities have so far failed all efforts to start a program in the much desired area of medicine (mostly due to their inability to fulfill the demanding quality requirements), private polytechnics have been quite successful in the development of programs (e.g.,

Table 8.2 Total enrollments in public and private institutions by disciplinary area, 2004/05

Scientific area	Private sector				Public sector			
	Polytechnic		University		Polytechnic		University	
	Number	%	Number	%	Number	%	Number	%
Education	7,874	25.0	888	1.3	9,840	9.1	14,326	8.2
Arts and Humanities	1,539	4.9	5,410	8.0	5,614	5.2	20,095	11.6
Social Sc., Law	5,436	17.2	34,654	51.6	30,271	27.9	49,110	28.2
Sciences, Informatics	776	2.5	3,325	5.0	1,755	1.6	23,126	13.3
Engineering, Manufacturing and Building Industries	868	2.8	9,830	14.6	32,937	30.4	39,444	22.7
Agriculture	0	0.0	315	0.5	2,956	2.7	4,505	2.6
Health and Social Protection	14,278	45.3	8,316	12.4	17,880	16.5	14,727	8.5
Services	736	2.3	4,419	6.6	7,123	6.6	8,564	4.9
Total	31,507	100.0	67,157	100.0	108,376	100.0	173,897	100.0

Source: Ministry of Science, Technology and Higher Education—OCES (2005).

nursing and health technologies). This has allowed private polytechnics to reduce programs in areas where the labor market was saturated, such as management and teacher training, which was compensated by increasing enrollments in the health sector.

These patterns of strong geographical and disciplinary concentration have created significant competition between institutions, especially private ones, with strong isomorphic effects. When an institution starts a new program that attracts students, many other institutions seize this opportunity and propose new similar programs irrespective of the absence of consolidated academic staff, facilities or libraries. Since they are competing for the same local pool of candidates, this has fostered waves of competition in several fields. There has been the "management" race, the "environment" race, and more recently the "health" race. However, this is apparently a short-term strategy as the niches rapidly become overpopulated and soon the institutions are pressed to find alternatives.

Financial Constraints

Another factor that has been fostering competition on the supply side has been funding, especially in the public sector. Government funds continue to be by far the major source of revenue for public universities. In recent years there has however been a noticeable increase in the relative share of tuition fees and some signs of diversification. The large value of "own resources" is explained by the inclusion of net balances from previous years, which became private revenue for

regulations replace collective decision-making by centralization of power in individual decision-makers. Another major change has been the reduction of the size of the main decision bodies (both at the central and lower levels). The new rules also reduce student participation and increase the participation of the outside community in institutional governance (making it compulsory in the central government body of each institution).

Another major change brought by the new legal framework is the possibility of a public institution adopting public foundation status. This requires government approval. Evidence is needed of the institution's capacity to raise half of its annual income through sources other than government's transfer through the funding formula. Moreover, the institution has to justify the strategic relevance of the change through a five-year development plan negotiated with the ministry.

The main advantages for the institution are the possibility of less uncertainty in the level of public funding and in mid-term planning. There are also some specific differences regarding the degree of financial autonomy, namely the possibility of borrowing money up to a certain limit, which has been denied until now to public institutions. The main disadvantage seems to be the fear that governments will feel less responsible for the funding of these institutions and that they will face significant pressure to find alternative sources of income and to rethink their priorities on the basis of their financial returns (and the organizational and institutional implications of those forces).

It may be worth noting in this context that most of the regulations defined for the other public institutions also apply to public foundations. The only major difference is the introduction of a Board of Trustees (for foundations). The Trustees are proposed by the University's general council and approved by the Ministry. However, most of the Board's duties correspond to ministerial responsibilities that are transferred to that body and do not seem to interfere with daily management, at least in nominal terms. Thus, even when introducing this experiment in the system, the government is quite cautious in the institutional variability it is allowing.

Another important issue when analyzing governmental interference and institutional autonomy refers to academic staff issues. In Portugal, as in most of Continental Europe, the qualifications of the personnel of public institutions, the definition of their employment conditions, and their career and salaries are all established in law, as both teaching and non-teaching staff are civil servants. Hence the degree of freedom institutions have in deploying staff is rather limited, being restricted by the legal framework applied to civil servants. Academic careers are still regulated by legal documents that were published in the late 1970s in the case of the universities (1979) and in the early 1980s for the polytechnic sub-system (1981), though they are scheduled to change soon.

It is not possible for each institution to negotiate individual salaries, specific duties or possible benefits. Moreover, it is almost impossible to hire a specific academic, paying each according to quality, skills and competencies. Whilst the creation of new foundations may have created an opportunity for greater institutional autonomy in staff management, the law defined that all staff members would preserve their civil servant status. Institutions may create parallel careers with different conditions, though only for new staff members or those renouncing their civil service status. This caution may be explained by the willingness to remove resistance to that change, since the decision to move to foundation status had to be approved in a committee elected for that purpose in each institution with a majority of faculty members (12 out of 21).

The situation may change in the near future, but once again it is being spearheaded by changes in the public sector and in the macro-structure of the Civil Service. Since the beginning of 2009, large parts of the public administration have changed their working conditions, one of the most important changes being the extinction of lifetime contracts. Thus, academic and non-academic staff now have individual work contracts, much closer to the prevailing situation in the private sector.

European Trends and National Peculiarities—Accreditation, Bologna and Trust

One of the major recent changes in Portuguese higher education refers to the evaluation and quality system where recent transformations represent an obvious loss of trust in institutions. The initial developments on quality assessment seem to correspond to Neave's (1994, 1996) law of anticipated results. In Portugal, the first quality assurance activities were an initiative of the Portuguese Council of Rectors (CRUP) that organized in 1993 a pilot experiment following the Dutch methodology. The Quality Assessment Act, Law 38/94, of 21 November 1994, passed by the Parliament, followed closely the CRUP's proposal and entrusted the ownership of the quality agency to "representative institutions", similar to the Dutch VSNU (Amaral and Rosa, 2004). The first round of assessments was completed in 1999 and included only the public universities and the Catholic University. The public polytechnics and the private higher education institutions have taken some time to join this process.

In the early 2000s some erosion of trust was already visible due to the lack of consequences of the system, despite public awareness that the very fast expansion of the higher education system had gone alongside some decline in quality. In 2002, a new Minister publicly complained that the conclusions of the external reports were obscure, and decided to change the system. Law 1/2003 was passed by Parliament on 6th January, clarifying the consequences of the results of the assessment, determining the rating of the evaluated programs, and introducing the concept of academic accreditation. The Minister, by forcing the quality agency to produce an accreditation-type conclusion—a yes or no answer— wanted a sounder basis for acting. However, the Minister did not stay long in office, the law was never regulated and accreditation was quickly forgotten.

In 2005, the new government commissioned the European Association for Quality Assurance in Higher Education (ENQA) to undertake a review of the quality assurance system and announced during the review process that the existing system would be dismantled and replaced by a new accreditation system in early 2007. Following the ENQA (2006) report the government prepared a law proposal that was passed by Parliament as Law 38/2007 of 16th August defining the legal framework for the new system. Later, the Government passed the Decree-Law 369/2007 of 5th November creating the new quality agency as a Foundation under private law, fully independent of both the government and institutions. The agency will be responsible for the evaluation and accreditation of both the institutions and their study programs. The new agency must comply with the European Standards and Guidelines for Quality Assurance (ESG) and become a member of the European register.

Another major change that shaped the Portuguese higher education system, as most of its European counterparts, has to do with the implications of the Bologna process. The types of degrees and diplomas and the definition of which institutions could award them were established in a Parliament Act—Law 46/86, of 14th October. To implement Bologna it was necessary to change this Act, which proved a difficult task, the process dragging on while some heated public debates took place (Veiga and Amaral, 2009).

What is interesting is that in Portugal the legal framework passed to implement the Bologna process was used, contrary to all expectations and debates, to clarify and reinforce the binary system, by creating conditions to increase the vocational emphasis of polytechnics and the research and scientific emphasis of universities. Only universities are allowed to confer third cycle degrees (doctorates) and integrated Master's. The second cycles of polytechnics have a vocational character, including in general a professional internship while in universities the second cycle includes a thesis and has a more scientific character.

There are obvious homogenizing tendencies in the Bologna process, at least in the convergence to a structure of BA–MA–PhD and in the use of instruments such as the European Qualifications Framework and programs such as the Tuning project. In Portugal, although public universities traditionally had substantial freedom to create new programs, the legislation allowing for the implementation of Bologna had a very severe restriction: the adaptation of an old program to the Bologna structure could only originate a single first cycle. However, despite this restriction, institutions were allowed to exercise their imagination when offering other study cycles. The effect of the new Accreditation Agency on the diversity of the system remains to be seen.

Concluding Remarks

For many years, economic arguments have been used to justify the usefulness of market forces as a tool to promote a better system of higher education (Wolf,

1993; Le Grand and Bartlett, 1993). Governments have been more willing to listen to those arguments when it comes to the part of competition. The idea of having institutions and individuals competing through financial or better human resources or students has been quite appealing for many policymakers, because they tend to believe that these competitive stimuli will make higher education not only more efficient, but also more effective in responding to social and economic needs. Competition has been regarded as a force that will stimulate higher education institutions to perform their missions more effectively.

In this chapter we have analyzed some recent trends in Portuguese higher education in order to assess if there has been a strengthening of market forces. There has been a clear strengthening of inter-institutional competition, stimulated in recent years by both the supply and the demand sides. On the latter, it is clear that sluggish student demand and an aversion to geographical mobility (especially due to increasing cost-sharing), have created a context in which institutions have to struggle to secure enough candidates to fill their *numerus clausus*. These competitive trends have been reinforced by a tendency of the supply side to be concentrated from both a geographical and a disciplinary point of view. In a time of increasing financial restrictions and declining demand, institutions have shown a significant tendency toward isomorphism and aversion to risk.

However, these competitive trends have been accompanied at the system level by a strengthening of regulation. Some of the most important cases refer to how the Bologna process was implemented in Portugal and also to the recent changes in quality evaluation, with the introduction of accreditation. Moreover, and despite the recommendations of the recent OECD (2007), Higher Education Review the subsequent legal and regulatory changes have seldom enlarged the managerial and financial autonomy of institutions, even when new legal possibilities were created such as public foundation status. Although some of these initiatives were presented in New Public Management garments, the actual changes suggest a strong regulatory approach. Overall, it seems that either the government does not trust institutions sufficiently to grant them significant powers in those respects, or it believes that government regulation may be a more effective way of attaining some of the system's objectives.

This combination of significant competition and strong government regulation poses interesting challenges to institutions and the coming years may be crucial to assess to what extent we will see a reshaping of the Portuguese higher education system. It is not difficult to imagine that the peculiar combination of competition and coordination will contribute to a situation in which institutions will face very different academic and financial situations. It is also likely that competition and policy guidance will lead some institutions, normally the weaker ones, to narrow their missions and to become essentially teaching institutions. Other institutions may be favored by a concentration of some streams of funding, especially as regards research. If this turns out to be the case, the Portuguese system may be evolving to a process of *marketization* mainly through segmentation where some groups of institutions will be formed with significant competition within the group, but very limited competition between the groups. It will be very interesting to see the extent to which this will be spearheaded by government coordination. If it is, it would be yet another example of governments playing with some aspects of marketization, namely inter-institutional competition, in order to shape the system according to certain political priorities, rather than the interests of the system as a whole.

References

Amaral, A. & Rosa, M. J. (2004) Portugal: professional and academic accreditation–the impossible marriage? In Schwarz, S. & Westerheijden, D. (Eds) *Accreditation and Evaluation in the European Higher Education Area*. Dordrecht: Kluwer Academic Press, pp. 127–57.

Amaral, A. & Teixeira, P. N. (2000) The rise and fall of the private sector in Portuguese higher education? *Higher Education Policy*, 13(3): 245–66.

European Association for Quality Assurance in Higher Education (ENQA). (2006) *Quality Assurance of Higher Education in Portugal*. Helsinki, ENQA Occasional Paper 10.

Department for Planning and Research (GPEARI). (2008) *Statistics on Portuguese Higher Education and Research*. Lisbon: Ministry for Science, Technology and Higher Education.

National Institute of Statistics (INE). (2008) *Portuguese Statistical Yearbook (Sine Datum)*. Lisbon: National Institute for Statistics (INE).

Le Grand, J. & Bartlett, W. (1993) *Quasi-Markets and Social Policy*. London: Macmillan Press.

Neave, G. (1996) Homogenization, integration and convergence: the Cheshire Cats of Higher Education analysis. In Van Meek, L., Goedegebuure, L., Kivinen, O. & Rinne, R. (Eds) *The Mockers and the Mocked: Comparative Perspectives on Differentiation, Convergence and Diversity in Higher Education*. London: Pergamon Press, pp. 26–41.

—— (1994) The policies of quality: development in higher education in Western Europe 1992–94, *European Journal of Education*, 29(2): 115–34.

Nunes, A. S. (2000) *Antologia Sociológica*. [Sociological Anthology] Lisboa: ICS.

Observatory for Science and Higher education (OCES). (2005) *Statistics on Portuguese Education and Research (Sine Datum)*. Lisbon: Ministry for Science, Technology and Higher Education.

Organisation for Economic Co-operation and Development (OECD). (2007) *Reviews of National Policies for Education: Tertiary Education in Portugal*, Paris: Organisation for Economic Co-operation and Development.

Simão, J. V., Santos, S. M. & Costa, A. A. (2002) *Ensino Superior: Uma Visão para a Próxima Década*, [Higher education: A Vision for the Next Decade] Lisboa: Gradiva.

Teixeira, P. N. & Amaral, A. (2007) Waiting for the tide to change? Strategies for survival of Portuguese private HEIs. *Higher Education Quarterly*, 61(2): 208–22.

Teixeira, P. N., Dill, D. D., Jongbloed, B. & Amaral, A. (Eds). (2004) *The Rising Strength of Markets in Higher Education*. Kluwer: Dordrecht.

Teixeira, P. N., Rosa, M. J. & Amaral, A. (2006) A broader Church? Expansion, access and cost-sharing in Portuguese Higher Education. In Teixeira, P. N., Johnstone, B., Rosa, M. J. & Vossensteyn, H. (Eds) *Cost-Sharing and Accessibility in Higher Education: A Fairer Deal?* Dordrecht: Springer, pp. 241–64.

Teixeira, P. N., Fonseca, M., Tavares, D. A., Sá, C. & Amaral, A. (2009) A regional mismatch? Student applications and institutional responses in the Portuguese public Higher Education system. In Mohrman, K., Shi, J., Feinblatt, S. E. & Chow, K. W. (Eds) *Public Universities and Regional Development*. Sichuan University Press, pp. 59–80.

Veiga, A. & Amaral, A. (2009) Survey on the implementation of the Bologna process in Portugal. *Higher Education*, 57(1): 57–69.

Wolf Jr, C. (1993) *Markets or Governments: Choosing between Imperfect Alternatives*. Cambridge, MA: MIT Press.

9

Diversification and Competition in the German Higher Education System

LYDIA HARTWIG

Introduction

During the past 10 years, the German higher education system has undergone a spate of reforms with the aim of enhancing its international competitiveness. To this end, institutions were gradually granted more autonomy in financial, organizational and staffing matters. They could select their students, and some Länder introduced tuition fees. Even though it is a federal system, the Federation and the Länder agreed on funding the Excellence Initiative, which broke the assumption that all universities were equal, and agreed on a federalism reform which allows competition between the 16 Länder regarding funding, students, researchers, pay scales and so forth. These developments and their impact will now be outlined.

Overall Size of System: Types of Institutions, Students, Admission and Degrees

Types of Institutions

Higher education in Germany is offered at three main types of institution: universities and equivalent institutions (including technical, pedagogical and theological institutions), universities of applied sciences (including institutions for public administration), and colleges of art and music. Universities usually offer a broad range of programs in all subjects and they have the right to award the doctorate (*Promotion*) and to train junior researchers. Universities of applied sciences have a practice-oriented bias in teaching and an integrated semester of practical training in a workplace (Lohmar and Eckhardt, 2009: 151–52). They concentrate on engineering sciences, economics, and social work. An increasing number of programs are organized as a dual system of academic studies and vocational training. Universities of applied sciences were initially established as teaching organizations with no research functions, but now they do applied research and development in different degrees. Other tertiary institutions are business academies for business and engineering (*Berufsakademien and Fachschulen*), but they do not have the status of higher education institutions.

Table 9.1 Number of higher education institutions and students according to type of institution in the winter semester 2007/08

Type of institution	Number of institutions		Number of students	
Universities and equivalent institutions	124	32%	1,338,556	69.0%
Universities of applied sciences	215	55%	572,330	29.4%
Colleges of art and music	52	13%	30,519	1.6%
Total	391	100%	1,941,405	100%

Source: Statistisches Bundesamt, Fachserie 11, Reihe 4.1, www.destatis.de.

Number of Institutions and Students

According to the Federal Statistical Office, there were 391 higher education institutions in the winter semester 2007/08, among them 124 universities, 215 universities of applied sciences and 52 colleges of art and music. The majority of students are enrolled at universities. Only about 30 percent of students attend a university of applied sciences.

In the winter semester 2007/08 there were 1,941,405 students in total, 926,644 of whom were female (48 percent), and 233,606 (12 percent) of whom were foreigners (the most frequent home countries are China and Turkey).

Public and Non-Public Higher Education

Most students are enrolled at public institutions. They can choose from a variety of universities with distinctive profiles and other institutions with a strong focus on vocational education. Distance teaching is provided by the Distance University of Hagen. Although private higher education has developed multifariously in recent years, and one-third of higher education institutions meanwhile are private or church-run, this development has had little quantitative effect. In 2006, only about 4 percent of all German students attended a private higher education institution (Statistische Ämter des Bundes und der Länder, 2008: 79). Private institutions usually concentrate on teaching and offer courses with a vocational bias. The Länder have the authority to award state-recognition to non-public institutions. This is dependent on proof that the private higher education institution is of equivalent status and follows equivalent quality standards. This is achieved through institutional accreditation carried out by the German Council of Science and Humanities.

Admission

Admission at universities requires a general qualification for university entrance (Allgemeine Hochschulreife—Abitur) which permits access to university programs without subject-specific restriction, or an entrance qualification for universities of applied sciences (Fachhochschulreife) which permits access for all programs. People with vocational qualifications can likewise enroll at higher education institutions. Admission procedures have been decentralized in recent years. By now, there are no central admission procedures for most degree courses except for medical subjects, and institutions select most applicants themselves (BMBF, 2008a: 30). Overall selection criteria like the general higher education entrance qualification are increasingly supplemented by the results of a selection process carried out by individual universities.

Degrees

The following academic degrees can be awarded by higher education institutions:

- Diplom and Magister (depending on the type of subject)
- Bachelor and Master
- State Examination (mainly in law, medicine and teacher training degree programs)
- Doctorate (only at universities and equivalent institutions of higher education).

The traditional German "Diplom" and "Magister" will be replaced by Bachelor and Master awards from 2010 on, as stated in the Bologna Declaration. In 2008, 31 percent of all students were enrolled in Bachelor and Master programs (Hochschulrektorenkonferenz [HRK], 2008: 21). Subject to the "Structural Guidelines" adopted by the Standing Conference of the Ministers of Education and Cultural Affairs of the Länder (Kultusministerkonferenz [KMK], 2008), universities and universities of applied sciences can likewise offer Bachelor and Master programs. The guidelines lay down requirements for the structure and the length of programs based on the European Credit Transfer System (ECTS). Bachelor programs lead to a first-degree qualifying for entry into a profession. Master programs can either be research-oriented or practice-oriented. The Bologna process implies a fundamental change of structures, subject matters and examinations in the German system. The way it is implemented in Germany according to detailed guidelines is being criticized by student organizations and professors.

Accreditation

Before 1998, all new degree programs had to be authorized by the respective Länder ministries in charge of higher education. Subsequently, an independent Accreditation Council was set up for the new Bachelor's and Master's programs. This mainly works through accrediting agencies, authorizing them for a set period of time to accredit study programs (Lohmar and Eckhardt, 2009: 260). At present, there are six private, not-for-profit accreditation agencies: three of them are subject-specific and three have a regional focus. In the long run, the costly and resource-consuming "program accreditation" will be displaced by a review of institutional quality assurance, the so-called "system accreditation".

Governance: Levels of Responsibilities and Policies

Federal System

Under the Basic Law—the German constitution—the higher education sector is solely the responsibility of the 16 Länder. Consequently, the organization, administration and funding of higher education institutions are regulated in detail by Länder legislation. There is therefore competition between the Länder in various fields like funding, conditions and salaries for academic staff, centers of excellence, and the extent of autonomy and liberalization granted to institutions.

Federalism Reform

With the federalism reform adopted by the parliament in 2006—the most comprehensive amendment of the Basic Law in German history—the scope of the Federal Government's responsibilities in the field of education was reduced even more. As a consequence, the Federal Government merely bears responsibility for financial assistance for students and the funding of research institutions outside the higher education sector. However, the Basic Law still enables particular forms of cooperation between the Federal Government and the Länder in cases of supra-regional importance (the so called "joint tasks", Basic Law Article 91b, Paragraph 1), like the funding of research institutions and buildings outside the higher education sector as well as large-scale research projects and equipment (Lohmar and Eckhardt, 2009: 33).

Policy Instruments: The Excellence Initiative and Higher Education Pact

At present, the Federal Government and the Länder act together in two fields of policy with supra-regional importance: in launching the Excellence Initiative and in making the Higher Education Pact. The Excellence Initiative promotes outstanding science and research in Germany, in order to raise its visibility in the international scientific community. Organized by the German Research Council and the German Council of Science and Humanities, through a peer review process with international experts, the Excellence Competition selected excellent projects in three areas: 39 Graduate Schools, 37 Clusters of Excellence and 9 Institutional Strategies to promote top-level research. The Federal Government and the Länder will therefore provide 1.9 billion Euros from 2007 to 2011 and beyond that 2.7 billion Euros for the next round. Furthermore, the Federal Government and the Länder have agreed on a Higher Education Pact to cope with an increasing number of students. Within this pact, Bund and Länder are providing in equal parts a total sum of 1.1 billion Euros from 2007 to 2010 to enable higher education institutions to admit 91,370 additional entrants. A Higher Education Pact II from 2011 to 2015 will create places for 275,000 additional students and will be financed with 6.4 billion Euros.

Coordinating Bodies

The proceedings between the Federal Government and the Länder to put all these agreements into execution are complex and difficult. However, a number of long-standing commissions and intermediate organizations in higher education exist to balance and manage the wide range of interests and the various concerns of policy, research and administration (Lohmar and Eckhardt, 2009: 47–50; BMBF, 2008b: 48). The Joint Research Conference *(Gemeinsame Wissenschaftskonferenz, GWK)* is the coordinating body for research and science policy, and its members are the Ministers for Research and Finance of Bund and Länder. The German Council for Science and Humanities (*Wissenschaftsrat*) is an advisory body to the Federal Government and the Länder being composed of researchers and persons of high public standing on the one side, and representatives of the 16 Länder and the Federation on the other. The Standing Conference of the Ministers of Education and Cultural Affairs (*Kultusministerkonferenz, KMK*) brings together the ministers of the Länder responsible for education, higher education and cultural affairs.

Deregulation

Along with the overall reform of the public sector (Enders and Jongbloed, 2007) a spate of reforms has run through the German higher education system since the beginning of the 1990s, with the aim of enhancing its international competitiveness by means of deregulation. Deregulation has the purpose of strengthening the autonomy of higher education institutions and implies the implementation of new management and funding mechanisms (Küpper, 2003), more autonomy to take decisions in organizational and staffing matters (Hartwig, 2004: 8), and the freedom to select applicants.

Funding Mechanisms of Higher Education Institutions, Teaching and Research

Core Funding of Teaching and Research by the Länder

Because higher education institutions are maintained by the Länder, current expenditure for research and teaching—including running expenses, personnel costs and costs for larger investments and premises—are funded through the Länder budgets. This core funding ensures the responsibilities and services provided by the institutions in teaching and research. In recent years, various competitive funding mechanisms based on performance-related parameters like the number of students and graduates, the number of doctorates, level of third-party funds, achievements in equality, etc., have been introduced in all Länder (Küpper, 2003; Orr, 2007). As regards funds for buildings and large scale equipment, the 16 Länder will only have available an annual sum of 700 million Euros from the Federal Government until 2013 as a consequence of the federalism reform in 2006.

Tuition Fees

Since 2005 the Länder can decide on financial contributions from undergraduate students. Seven Länder made use of this option for the first time in 2007 by levying tuition fees ranging up to 500 Euro per semester. Tuition fees for long-term students and for an additional course of study are charged in most Länder. The revenue from tuition fees totaled 700 million Euros in 2007; this amounts to 4 percent of the total expenditure for higher education institutions, excluding medical institutions (Autorengruppe Bildungsberichterstattung, 2008: 32). Tuition fees must be used directly for the benefit of students. At the same time, student loan systems were developed and student loans are provided by federal state banks and a large number of private banks.

Student Maintenance

The main sources of funding for students' living expenses are financial support from their parents (90 percent of the student population receive money from their parents), students' own earnings (60 percent earn money from their jobs), and funding through the Federal Training Assistance Act *(Bundesausbildungsförderungsgesetz—BAFöG)*. Twenty-nine percent of the student body receives funding from the Federal Training Assistance Act (Hochschul-Informations-System GmbH, 2008: 17–18). Other sources like partner's income, grants or loans play a minor role.

Research Project Grants

Apart from the core funding by the Land, higher education institutions acquire third-party funds from the German Research Council (*Deutsche Forschungsgemeinschaft, DFG*), and other organizations and foundations for research and development, such as the European Union and industry. The DFG is the main funding body for research at universities and other publicly funded research institutions, providing all branches of research with project grants. In

2005, higher education institutions spent 44 percent of their total expenditure on research and development (9.2 billion Euros), 40 percent of this is funded by third-party funds (3.5 billion Euros) (BMBF, 2008b: 483–84).

Expenditure

Public expenditure of higher education institutions totaled 24.6 billion Euros in 2005 (Statistisches Bundesamt, 2008: 18–19). Ninety percent of the total was provided by the Länder. Public expenditure per student varies between Länder and subjects. Medical science features the highest running expenses, followed by natural and engineering sciences. According to OECD data, 85 percent of the total expenditure for higher education was financed by public sources and 15 percent was financed by private sources (OECD, 2008: 273).

Academic Staff, Duties, Employment and Pay

Teaching at universities is performed by professors, academic staff and specialized teaching staff (Lohmar and Eckhardt, 2009: 225). Professors and academic staff are practicing teaching and research in different degrees within their fields. Academic staff are mostly employed on contracts for a limited period of time with the aim of further qualification (see later, Academic Labor Market: Training); contracts and payments may vary. Universities have a large number of academic staff and their teaching capacities are important as most students are enrolled at universities (Autorengruppe Bildungsberichterstattung, 2008: 122). At the universities of applied sciences, with a relatively low proportion of research, teaching is predominantly performed by professors.

Professors are usually appointed by the respective Länder ministries as civil servants with limited or unlimited tenure, but they can also be employed as salaried employees. After a reform of salary structure in 2005, all newly appointed professors are now assigned to the salary classes W2 and W3 which implies a lower basic salary with the opportunity to receive performance bonuses. Junior professors are usually employed in W1 for a maximum of six years but there are tenure options.

Research Institutions Outside Higher Education and the Connection with Universities

Germany has a broad and differentiated landscape of science and innovation (BMBF 2008b: 47–50). The backbone of the German research system is traditionally the universities, due to the scope of their themes and methods and through their task of training junior researchers. Research at university comprehends a wide range of subjects, themes and methods. In addition, Germany has a large sector of non-university research. There are four outstanding research

It has been having outstanding effects on the entire higher education system and it will be continued. Another important objective is to reduce the time of qualification for junior academics, while ensuring more independence at a younger age and opening more secure career paths (Wissenschaftsrat, 2001: 79–82).

Conclusion

Continued reforms in the past years have strengthened the competitive character of the German higher education system. The introduction of market mechanisms has partially displaced central management and has led to a significant increase of autonomy in various fields like funding, governance, admission and accreditation. Moreover, the Excellence Initiative has broken the assumption that all universities are equal, bringing along new forms of cooperation between universities and non-university institutions. There are more challenges for the future: to provide funding for the increasing number of students and to improve the quality of teaching.

Note

1. Stifterverband is the business community's innovation agency for the German science system, see www.stifterverband.org

References

Autorengruppe Bildungsberichterstattung (Eds). (2008) *Bildung in Deutschland 2008: Ein indikatorengestützter Bericht mit einer Analyse zu Übergängen im Anschluss an den Sekundarbereich I.* Bildung in Deutschland. Bielefeld: Bertelsmann,. http://www.bildungsbericht.de/daten2008/bb_2008.pdf.

Bundesministerium Für Bildung Und Forschung (BMBF) (Ed.). (2007) *Research and Innovation in Germany 2007—In the mirror of statistics.* Bonn, Berlin: BMBF. http://www.bmbf.de/pub/research_and_innovation_2007.pdf.

—— (2008a) *Grund-und Strukturdaten 2007/2008: Daten zur Bildung in Deutschland.* Bonn, Berlin: BMBF. http://gus.his.de/ gus/download.html.

—— (2008b) *Bundesbericht Forschung und Innovation 2008.* Bonn, Berlin: BMBF. http://www.bmbf.de/de/12210.php.

—— (2008c) *Bundesbericht zur Förderung des wissenschaftlichen Nachwuchses (BuWiN).* Bonn, Berlin: BMBF. http://www.buwin.de/index.php?id = 301.

Enders, J. & Jongbloed, B. (2007) The public, the private and the good in Higher Education and research: an introduction. In Enders, J. & Jongbloed, B. (Eds) *Public-Private Dynamics in Higher Education: Expectations, Developments and Outcomes.* Science Studies. Bielefeld: transcript, pp. 9–36.

Frank, A., Meyer-Guckel, V. & Schneider, C. (Eds) (2007) *Innovationsfaktor Kooperation: Bericht des Stifterverbandes zur Zusammenarbeit zwischen Unternehmen und Hochschulen.* Essen: Edition Stifterverband. http://www.stifterverband.de/.

Hartwig, L. (2004) *National Report of Germany for the OECD/IMHE-HEFCE Project on Financial Management and Governance of Higher Education Institutions.* Monographien/Bayerisches Staatsinstitut für Hochschulforschung und Hochschulplanung N.F., 69. München: IHF. http://www.ihf.bayern.de/?Publikationen:Monographien.

Hochschul-Informations-System GmbH (Ed.). (2008) *Social and Economic Conditions of Student Life in Europe: Synopsis of Indicators. Final Report.* Eurostudent III 2005–2008. Bielefeld: Bertelsmann.

Hochschulrektorenkonferenz (HRK) (Ed.). (2008) *Statistische Daten zur Einführung von Bachelor- und Masterstudiengängen, Wintersemester 2008/2009*. Bonn: Statistiken zur Hochschulpolitik 3/2008. http://www.hrk.de/de/download/dateien/HRK_StatistikBA_MA_WiSe2008_09_final_mit_Cover.pdf-.

Kultusministerkonferenz (KMK). (2008) *Ländergemeinsame Strukturvorgaben gemäß § 9 Abs. 2 HRG für die Akkreditierung von Bachelor-und Masterstudiengängen: Beschluss der Kultusministerkonferenz vom 10.10.2003 i.d.F. vom 07.02.2008*. www.kmk.org/fileadmin/pdf/dokumentation/BeschlKMK/Hochschulen_und_Wissenschaft/Laendergemeinsame_Strukturvorgaben.pdf-.

Küpper, H.-U. (2003) Management mechanisms and financing of higher education in Germany. *Higher Education Management and Policy* 15, no. 1 (2003): 71–89.

Lohmar, B. & Eckhardt, T. (2009) *The Education System in the Federal Republic of Germany 2007: A description of responsibilities, structures and developments in education policy for the exchange of information in Europe*. Bonn. http://www.kmk.org/dokumentation/das-bildungswesen-in-der-bundesrepublik-deutschland/dossier-englisch/publikation-zum-download.html.

Müller-Böling, D. (2000) *Die entfesselte Hochschule*. Gütersloh: Verl. Bertelsmann-Stiftung.

Organisation for Economic Cooperation and Development (OECD). (2008) *Education at a Glance 2008: OECD Indicators*, Paris: OECD.

Orr, D. (2007). More competition in German Higher Education: expectations, developments, outcomes. In Enders, J. & Jongbloed, B. (Eds) *Public-Private Dynamics in Higher Education: Expectations, Developments and Outcomes*. Science Studies. Bielefeld: transcript, pp. 157–184.

Sondermann, M., Dagmar, S., Scholz, A.-M. & Horborstel, S. (Eds) (2008) *Exzellenzinitiative: Beobachtungen aus der Implementierungsphase*. IFQ working paper 5. Bonn: IFQ.

Statistische Ämter Des Bundes Und Der Länder (2008) *Internationale Bildungsindikatoren im Ländervergleich, Ausgabe 2008*. Bundesamt.

Statistisches Bundesamt (2008) *Bildungsfinanzbericht: Im Auftrag des Bundesministeriums für Bildung und Forschung und der Ständigen Konferenz der Kultusminister der Länder in der Bundesrepublik*. Wiesbaden: Statistisches Bundesamt.

Wissenschaftsrat (2001) *Wissenschaftsrat, Personalstruktur und Qualifizierung: Empfehlungen zur Förderung des wissenschaftlichen Nachwuchses*, Köln: Wissenschaftsrat. http://www.wissenschaftsrat.de/Veroffentlichungen/veroffentlich.htm.

—— (2006) *Empfehlungen zum arbeitsmarkt-und demographiegerechten Ausbau des Hochschulsystems*. Köln: Wissenschaftsrat. http://www.wissenschaftsrat.de/Veroffentlichungen/veroffentlich.htm.

—— (2007a) *Empfehlungen zur Rolle und Künftigen Entwicklung der Bundeseinrichtungen mit FuE-Aufgaben*. Köln: Wissenschaftsrat, 2007. http://www.wissenschaftsrat.de/Veroffentlichungen/veroffentlich.htm.

—— (2007b) *Empfehlungen zur Interaktion von Wissenschaft und Wirtschaft*. Köln: Wissenschaftsrat. http://www.wissenschaftsrat.de/Veroffentlichungen/veroffentlich.htm.

—— (2007c) *Empfehlungen zu einer lehrorientierten Reform der Personalstruktur an Universitäten*. Köln: Wissenschaftsrat. http://www.wissenschaftsrat.de/Veroffentlichungen/ veroffentlich.htm.

10
Emerging Markets in the Finnish System

SEPPO HÖLTTÄ, TEA JANSSON AND JUSSI KIVISTÖ

Introduction

As is typical in Nordic countries, the role of state regulation in the higher education system has been strong in Finland. This long tradition of non-market
orientation seems ongoing, although the future reforms of higher education
policy are taking the system slowly but steadily toward a more market-oriented
approach.

System Overview

Institutions and Funding

The Finnish higher education system is a dual (or binary) system comprised of
universities and polytechnics. The 20 universities include 10 multi-faculty institutions, three schools of economics and business administration, three universities of technology, and four art academies, all offering Bachelor, Master,
Licentiate and Doctoral level degrees. All universities are public and state-
funded. According to the legislation, the purpose of universities is to promote
independent research and scientific knowledge and to provide the highest
education based on this research in their particular fields of study. Of the 26
polytechnics, six are run by local authorities, seven by municipal education consortia, and 13 by private organizations. Polytechnics carry out research and
development, which serve polytechnic education and support working life especially in engineering, business and health care. They play an important role in
regional development as providers of high-quality education and as developers
of the economic life of the regions, in particular of small- and medium-sized
enterprises. All polytechnics offer Bachelor and Master level polytechnic degrees
in selected fields (see, e.g., Eurybase, 2007). Polytechnic degrees are more voca-
tionally oriented and one of the requirements for applying to a polytechnic
Master degree is three years' relevant work experience.

The primary regulative agency for both universities and polytechnics is the Ministry of Education (MoE). MoE acts through resource allocation, legislation and information. Universities are governed by the *Universities Act* and polytechnics by the *Polytechnics Act* which provide the mission, overall administration and structure of the higher education institutions (HEIs). In addition, the government *Decree on Higher Education Degrees* lays down the status of each higher education degree. It determines the degrees to be awarded, their objectives and overall structure, the responsibilities of different HEIs in different fields of education and the degrees to be awarded (Ministry of Education, 2005: 71). The main policy guidelines and development targets are determined on a general level in the *Development Plan for Education and Research*, which is adopted by the government for a six-year period and revised every four years. Budgetary funds are allocated on the basis of a funding formula which is the most important tool for the MoE in regulating the operations of universities and polytechnics (Ministry of Education, 2005: 24).

In principle, degree instruction at all HEIs is free of charge for both domestic and foreign students. However, from the beginning of 2008, the government granted the right for universities and polytechnics to offer fee-based degree education on all degree levels for student groups coming from a country outside the European Economic Area. The condition is that this education is financed by organizations (e.g., foreign governments, foundations and companies), not by the individual students themselves. If the new legislation passes Parliament, HEIs will be provided the opportunity to charge tuition fees to individual students coming from non-EEA countries in Master programs taught in English. Universities and polytechnics themselves determine the level of fees, student selection and enrollment. Simultaneously, HEIs are required to establish scholarship funds to promote equity in these programs.

Students and Financial Support

In addition to tuition fee-free education, students benefit from a generous student aid system. Student aid comprises a much larger share of all public spending on tertiary education than in the average OECD member country (OECD, 2006: 51). State-supported student aid includes study grant, housing supplement and a state guarantee for private student loan. The criteria for granting student financial aid include admission to an educational institution, full-time study and need for financial assistance (Eurostudent, 2008).

Free education and substantial student aid together mean that Finnish higher education relies heavily on public funding. In 2005, public expenditure was 96.1 percent, the second highest percentage of all OECD countries (OECD average 73.1 percent). The proportion of private expenditure was 3.9 percent, the second lowest of all OECD countries (OECD average 26.9 percent) (OECD, 2008: 253). So far, endowments, donations, gifts and private sponsorship have been a relatively insignificant source of funding for HEIs, but this may change in the new legislative framework.

Students compete for study places, and particularly secondary education graduates have to queue to access their field of choice. About half of the applicants attain a study place in higher education. The ratio of demand to supply is, on average, substantially higher in the university sector than it is in the polytechnic sector (OECD, 2006: 12). However, there is great variance between study fields. Entry levels range from 5–10 percent in fine and performing arts to over 50 percent in some areas of engineering and applied sciences (e.g., pharmacy) (OECD, 2006: 12).

The total number of university students has remained constant, although a slight decrease may be anticipated as limitations to study times have been introduced for Bachelor and Master levels for students accepted after 2005 (see Table 10.1). The other Bologna-induced changes are the increase in students categorized as Bachelor students and the numbers of Bachelor degrees. Before the Master degree was considered as a basic university degree, but since 2008 all university students have had to transfer to the new two-cycle degree structure and obtain a Bachelor degree before the Master.

In the polytechnic sector, the experiment since 2002 and the official introduction of the Master level in 2005 has not yet contributed to student or degree numbers: the Bachelor degree continues to be the main polytechnic degree (see Table 10.2). The polytechnic Master degree has been planned as the main track for further studies for polytechnic Bachelor level graduates. For the future, MoE has set a target of increasing the number of Master students in polytechnics to 3800 in 2012.

Research and Funding

Finland's input into research and development (R&D) has grown substantially from the mid-1980s. The national innovation system has provided the framework for the research and higher education policy since the early 1990s. The coordination of the national innovation system is in the hands of the highest political leadership. The national science, technology and innovation policies are formulated by the *Science and Technology Policy Council*, which is chaired by the Prime Minister.

The *Academy of Finland*, the Finnish Research Council organization, takes care of central research administration and finances most university research. The Academy has four research councils, appointed for three-year terms, each financing research in its disciplines. Another important task for the Academy is to evaluate research. Public funding for technology and development is channeled through the Finnish Funding Agency for Technology Research (TEKES), which also plays a major part in the external funding of the universities (Ministry of Education, 2005: 24).

Table 10.1 Students and degrees in universities

Year	Total number of students	Master students	Bachelor students	Licenciate and Doctoral students	Total number of degrees	Bachelor degrees	Master degrees	Licentiate degrees	Doctorate degrees
2005	(173,175)	126,657	24,373	22,145	(17,788)	2,913	12,920	533	1,422
2006	(174,064)	108,395	43,770	21,899	(18,840)	3,814	13,128	489	1,409
2007	(173,753)	93,313	58,883	21,557	(21,749)	5,879	13,884	460	1,526
2008	(161,350)	44,549	96,009	20,792	(37,652)	13,876	21,825	425	1,526

Source: KOTA-database.

Table 10.2 Students and degrees in polytechnics

Year	Total number of students	Bachelor students	Master students	Total number of degrees	Bachelor degrees	Master degrees
2005	132,783	132,154	629	21,618	21,397	221
2006	132,560	131,185	1,375	21,156	21,006	150
2007	133,284	131,517	1,767	21,331	20,969	362
2008	132,501	130,508	1,993	21,800	21,120	680

Source: (Statistics Finland).

Table 10.3 Finnish R&D funding

Year	Total R&D funding in HEIs	Private R&D funding in HEIs	Public R&D funding in HEIs	Universities	Polytechnics	University hospitals
2004	€1.04 billion	€60.6 million	€871.5 million	€875.8 million	€89.8 million	€70.2 million
2005	€1.04 billion	€67.8 million	€859.3 million	€872.3 million	€99.6 million	€70.2 million
2006	€1.08 billion	€70.8 million	€886.8 million	€890.8 million	€107.4 million	€81 million
2007	€1.17 billion	€81.6 million	€948.8 million	€968.3 million	€117 million	€79.3 million

The HEI research support is divided into core funding and competitive funding. The former is well-suited to long-term infrastructure development, while the latter is usually of a time-limited nature and is less useful for the infrastructure. Most of the competitive funding is provided by the Finnish Academy and TEKES and is the part of the HEI support that has grown most in recent years. In 2007, the budget shares of these two main funding bodies were 16.3 percent (€309 million) and 30.3 percent (€575 million) (Statistics Finland, 2009). Core funding for HEIs, which includes expenses for both education and research, has increased less: in 2005, only 58 percent of the total support for HEIs was core funding, compared with 75 percent in 1996 (OECD, 2006: 25). In 2007, national spending on R&D was 3.5 percent of the GDP, which is one of the highest in the OECD countries. The universities got the greatest share of this, while hospitals and polytechnics received less. However, the R&D expenditures at polytechnics have grown rapidly in recent years, from only €27 million in 1999 to €117 million in 2007 (Statistics Finland, 2009; cf. OECD, 2006).

The Development of the Finnish Higher Education System

Policies and Market Forces

Even in the late 1980s, Finland had one of the most centrally controlled higher education systems in Europe. Expansion and regional decentralization had been the main policy goals from the 1960s through the 1980s. The new higher education policy, which reflected the national priority given to higher education and research, in the form of a guarantee of financial growth was formally initiated as the *Higher Education Development Act 1987–1996*. This laid down the basis for the development of new steering instruments and accountability measures to the state to replace the direct control machinery (Hölttä, 1988: 96–102).

A remarkable policy change took place in the early and mid-1990s. The change was characterized by a shift from general expansion policy toward focused policy, in which higher education policy was closely integrated with economic and industrial policies. HEIs were given new social roles as the major institutions of the national and regional innovation systems.

Since the 1990s, the core of steering and planning has been based on *steering-by-results*. In the performance agreement, the goals for the institution and funding are agreed upon and target outcomes are set for a three-year period. The targets are reviewed and confirmed and resources are determined annually by the representatives of the Ministry and the Rector. This agreement is based on the national policy goals which are derived from the national *Development Plan for Higher Education and Research*, the three-year plans of the universities, and the universities' offers concerning the institutional goals (Ministry of Education, 2004: 9). A similar planning and contracting system is applied in the polytechnic sector.

The most important targets for universities are the annual average numbers of Master and PhD degrees awarded during the contract period. Development programs and projects of national importance, aiming at the implementation of national policy programs, are also agreed upon in these contracts. The fact that the agreements are made for a three-year period provides the institutions with additional flexibility. Therefore, only marginal issues are negotiated and agreed upon for the following years of the contract.

Both sectors in the dual system have a reasonable degree of autonomy at present, compared with some other systems (OECD, 2006: 68). This autonomy is guaranteed by national legislation (The Universities Act, Polytechnics Act) and in the case of universities, by the State Constitution. Especially from the perspective of constitutional and legislative protection of academic freedom, Finnish universities and academics seem to enjoy a high level of academic freedom compared to the other 23 EU countries (see Karran, 2007). Universities officially have the power to allocate internally the budget as they wish. Within their financial autonomy, universities can conclude agreements, acquire external funding and use income generated through external funding. Universities themselves make decisions concerning their facilities. They do not own the premises they use, most are leased from the state-owned real estate company. Nevertheless, universities may also rent premises from commercial providers (Ministry of Education, 2005: 72).

There are, however, several issues which restrict actual autonomy. In addition to the fact that HEIs cannot collect tuition fees from individual students, the present legal status of universities as "state accounting offices" constrains their flexibility in financial matters, for instance by prohibiting them from acquiring loans from credit grantors. Even though universities and polytechnics cannot collect tuition fees from individual students studying for a degree, they have been recently allowed to enter the international educational market in a limited way. As mentioned earlier, the government recently granted the right to charge for degree education for groups from non-EEA countries. So far, HEIs have actually not offered this type of training.

In the future, the financial autonomy of universities will be strengthened through changes in their legal status. New legislation will extend their opportunities to operate in the consumer and capital markets. From the perspective of accounting, universities will be separated from the government budget, which has two implications. First, the bulk of university revenues will continue to come from government but in the form of a subsidy rather than a direct allocation through the annual budget. Second, the way universities hold and apply cash assets will also be different. At present, all university funds are held in Treasury accounts: universities only have access to the money needed to meet that day's commitments. In one sense, therefore, universities have not had to consider cash flow but they will have to do so from January 1st, 2010 when the available money will comprise unspent grants at the end of 2009, plus a pro-rated share from a special government allocation (Dobson, 2008). Premises and buildings will also be transferred from the government to three new commercial companies which will be partially owned by universities and the government.

Characteristics of Finnish System as a Market and Non-Market System

Institutional Governance and Labor Markets

As stated earlier, Finnish HEIs are in many respects self-governing, determining the contents of their programs, admission and student numbers, but the autonomy of HEIs is constrained by the fact that establishing a new field of education, subject or educational program is based on the decision of the MoE. Universities are not allowed to initiate degree-based training in new disciplinary fields (e.g., Engineering, Medical Science, Law) without the approval of the MoE. The purpose of this restriction is to ensure national coordination and the quality of the programs within the scope of the HEIs' educational responsibilities and the resources available to them. This is quite typical for state-funded systems, where study places or degrees are the central resource allocated according to the labor market needs' forecast. This is analogous to the old welfare state ideology, where forecasting labor (market) demands played an important role due to the qualification requirements for many (public) professions, where university degrees have traditionally functioned as a screening device. These forecasts of labor market needs, adjusted to reflect policy targets for the government, become the basis for a national Development Plan, that provides the framework for education supply. The Development Plan also provides the framework within which negotiations between the MoE and individual institutions take place. Enrollment and degree targets for each field of education are agreed between them, and contained in each HEI's performance agreement with the MoE (OECD, 2006: 11).

Because of excess demand, institutions do not engage in a fierce competition for students, although institutions and fields of education aspire to retain a level of desirability and thus selectivity. In the Finnish system, resource allocation is not driven by student demands, but according to the labor market demands forecast. This is clearly an obstacle for HEIs to respond to labor market demand without the permission of centralized planning office, MoE. The forecast labor market activity has been assigned a major role in the allocation of resources.

Pricing of education in HEIs is basically non-existent due to the absence of tuition fees. In R&D activities, HEIs have recently started to develop their accounting and cost-calculation practices so that they can determine market prices for their contracted R&D projects. However, the new higher education legislation enables HEIs to collect tuition fees from individual Master students coming from non-EEA countries. This means that pricing and cost calculation will be increasingly important activities for the HEIs in the future. Nevertheless, it remains to be seen how Finnish HEIs will exploit these new opportunities. Finland is unlikely to establish a large presence in the global student market, owing to reasons of location, weather and language; hence these tuition fees are unlikely to have significant impact on the overall balance of public and private resources in the tertiary system. Nonetheless, they may have a beneficial effect on the incentives activating HEIs, providing them with stronger inducements and more substantial resources with which to engage in the targeted and selective recruitment of non-EEA students and assisting other activities through cross-subsidization (OECD, 2006: 56).

Academic Labor Market

Academic labor markets are quite poorly developed in Finland because universities have not had freedom to decide on salaries. The formal status of the faculty of universities is that of civil servants. This status implies both a primacy of state collective bargaining processes for salaries and conditions of service, but also a potential lack of maneuver and management discretion at institutional level (OECD, 2006: 58). Within the scope of the collective labor agreements, the universities have full decision powers in hiring personnel and appointing professors. Universities have full autonomy in electing their Rectors, Boards and other administrative bodies (Ministry of Education, 2005: 72). Among other groups of civil servants, university staff have been included to new performance-based salary system from 2006. Instead of the former seniority-basis, in the new system salary consists of two components: demand level (job requirements) and the employee's performance (see, e.g., Kekäle, 2008). New legislation will also allow universities some discretion in determining the work terms and conditions, and the civil servant status of staff will be replaced with ordinary employment contracts. Different models of salary systems are applied in the polytechnic sector, depending on the legal status of the maintaining organization and the collective bargaining contract.

Finnish universities have not been able to use financial rewards in recruitment, so that institutions have quite restricted means to compete on talent. It is not uncommon for a (Master) graduate from a department to proceed to Doctoral studies in the same department and finally obtain employment there (OECD, 2006: 26). The career flexibility and operation of academic labor markets are constrained by the absence of proper tenure tracks, only a few new professorial posts are available each year. The mobility of Finnish HEI staff is not only low within the country, it is also low internationally. Only about 7 percent of the PhD students in Finland are foreigners and academic staff members are rarely recruited from abroad (OECD, 2006: 26).

The established performance-based salary system has, however, been the first step toward increased flexibility and competition in universities. Further, opening academic labor markets to international markets has been a special concern in the country. The Finland Distinguished Professor (FiDiPro) program is a new funding program jointly launched by the Academy of Finland and the National Technology Agency (TEKES) with the aim of recruiting professor-level top researchers, either foreign researchers or Finnish researchers who have long worked abroad.

In 2007, there were nearly 79,500 persons employed in R&D in Finland. Over half of the research personnel worked for business enterprises and 22,560 in the field of higher education. In universities the teaching staff was 7,785 in 2008, of whom 2,269 were professors. As a result of the establishment of the Graduate School system, the annual numbers of PhDs has increased in both quantity and quality (as well as in equality) in recent years, from 765 (37 percent women) in 1995 to 1,526 (55 percent women) in 2008 (Statistics Finland, 2009; KOTA Online, 2009).

Competition and Student Markets

The Finnish system is a non-market system also on the grounds of low competition. In principle, students as "consumers" have a wide choice of supplier, since higher education is tuition-free and enrolling at a university or a polytechnic is not in any way regulated according to place of residence. Students have multiple suppliers offering a wide variety of programs from which to choose. Within HEIs, students have relative freedom to choose subjects and studies within their degrees. Most institutions have flexible learning agreements so that students can take courses in other institutions if the subject is not offered in their home institution and the studies fit their planned degree. Thus students have freedom to choose their program. On the other hand, *numerus clausus* is in use for all institutions for almost all fields. Freedom of choice is constrained by the fact that all of the Finnish HEIs are public. A further obstacle is that the applicants may only accept one study place leading to a higher education degree in each academic year (Eurybase, 2007: 90).

Finnish higher education policy has long been based on a non-competitive "equal but different" approach, where the aim is to minimize resourcing differences between HEIs. The system strives to keep the student markets separate for the university and polytechnic sector. The distinction, however, is becoming blurred for several reasons (OECD, 2006: 11). There is a level of academic drift, which is increased by the higher education reform which will more directly equate the polytechnic degrees with the university Bachelor degrees. Similarly, the recent introduction of the polytechnic Master degree has vitiated the distinction between the two sectors. It may be anticipated that as the two sectors become similar also the labor markets will become more integrated.

However, provider freedom is still heavily regulated with practically no freedom of entry of new suppliers. Since the government has the formal power to grant official approval for new institutions, the degrees of the new providers are not recognized (Välimaa, 2004: 112). This also means that the institutions and their degrees not mentioned in legislation have no possibility to receive funding from the government. Second, given the practically tuition fee-free policy of public universities and the relatively high access rate, there is no market for fee-collecting private institutions.

In general, Finnish students have good information concerning the availability of programs and their acceptance rates through the websites and admission guides of institutions. There is no demand for price information in the absence of tuition fees. Basically, the only "price information" students may need is the indirect costs of study (housing rents and other living costs, fees of public transportation, etc.) but even these are more or less meaningless factors due to the student support system (subsidized meals and public transportation, and housing supplement). According to the OECD reviewers, the most significant factor constraining efficient student choice in Finland is the limited information regarding the quality of degree programs. They frankly state that the quality assurance system may not be able to provide systematic and comparable information about the quality of HEIs (OECD, 2006: 47). This can be seen as a consequence of the national quality assurance system, which emphasizes voluntary quality improvement by HEIs instead of accountability and control (see, e.g., Ministry of Education, 2005: 77–80).

University students can have some information regarding institutions through the open access database KOTA Online (https://kotaplus.csc.fi/online)

(UNDP, 2007). In other words, the market evaluation of first degree holders is relatively low, even though almost half of all graduates complete their education with this degree only. The second division, between traditional and all other institutions, means in practice that the most valuable degrees—those with highest wage premia and in traditionally most lucrative areas—are from a handful of institutions, almost exclusively public, located in major academic cities, such as Warsaw and Cracow, followed by Poznan, Wroclaw, Lodz and Gdansk. Finally, as private institutions are teaching-only institutions (i.e., they neither possess prestige, nor are able to seek it); they provide non-restrictive access, with 80 percent of them offering first degrees only, and 80 percent of their student body being part-time; their degrees, in general, are less valuable in the labor market.

In terms of subjects offered, private institutions were more active in responding to new demands of the labor market (and of students themselves) in the first half of the 1990s—when public institutions were still unable to respond to emergent market realities—but many of them have been offering poorly taught and undemanding degrees in "popular and cheap-to-run" fields of studies, as an OECD economic survey of Poland recently put it (OECD, 2006: 106). In 2007, 26 percent of graduates from both sectors were in economics and administration, 15 percent in educational studies, 15 percent in social sciences, and 8 percent in humanities; only 5.4 percent of graduates were in science and technical/engineering areas (GUS, 2008: 24) The structure of graduates from the private sector is much less differentiated, with the share in economics and administration reaching over 50 percent.

Turning toward the Market: Increasing Financial Self-Reliance

In both scholarly research (e.g., Shattock, 2005) and policy documents, new management, organizational and financial options suggested to public higher education systems are increasingly related to three notions (and phenomena): academic entrepreneurialism (in teaching, research and third mission activities); financial self-reliance (and significantly smaller dependence of academic institutions on core state funding); and cost-sharing (in introducing, or increasing, tuition fees, accompanied by more student loans and fewer student scholarships, etc.) (Shattock, 2005; Williams, 2003; Johnstone, 1998, 2007; Kwiek, 2009c). In Poland these are combined with internal (public sector) and external (new private providers) privatization. All these three notions (and phenomena) introduce strong market mechanisms to educational systems and figure prominently in recent national and EU-level debates on financially sustainable higher education in Europe. At the same time, the three dimensions are highly contentious issues for most university stakeholders, including policy makers, students, and academics. We have studied academic entrepreneurialism with respect to Poland elsewhere (Kwiek, 2008a, 2008b). Let us only note here that the role of teaching-related entrepreneurialism in both public and private sectors is very important but entrepreneurialism in research is restricted to top selected institutions in the public sector.

Financial self-reliance of institutions raises an interesting question about its impact on the changing relationships between the three missions of Polish universities: teaching, research and service to society. Overall, public universities in Poland in the last 15 years seem to have been gradually losing their commitment to the research mission and to be becoming increasingly teaching-oriented institutions. This move will have dire consequences for the quality of courses, curricula and research. In fact, the directions of evolution of top Western European and top Polish universities seem divergent (for the former, see Kaiser et al., 2003; Schwarzenberger, 2008; Leyden, 2005; OECD, 2008). Not surprisingly, one of the major OECD concerns is that while Polish HE has been financially "squeezed to the point of serious damage" (OECD, 2007: 118) institutions still do not even consider external sources of funding,

> most institutions interpret the advice to become more entrepreneurial as an invitation to sell core educational service to as many students as the law permits, and do not see the need to look for new sources of revenue.
>
> (OECD, 2007: 57)

While the evolution of the Polish system so far seems to show general similarities compared to most Western European ones, it also shows a substantial difference in institutional focus: research-intensity of top Western universities and teaching-intensity of top Polish universities (see OECD, 2004; 2008: 163–258; Kwiek, 2009a). The divergent evolution reveals a major weakness of Polish higher education in general. New ministerial policy intends to change the direction: a basic feature of a new model of higher education is "the promotion of the culture of getting competitive funds" (MoSHE, 2009: 27).

There are several lessons to be drawn for Poland from countries in which, first, huge expansion was driven by ever-growing demand, and then the expansion was stopped by both changing demographics and relative saturation of the student market. It is possible that a combination of several conditions—the (probable) introduction of fees for full-time students in the public sector or (conceivable) state subsidization of private institutions for their teaching services, further diversification of the study offer in the private sector and its further regional diversification, and higher quality of teaching (conceivable)—might lead to more fully fledged competition between the two sectors in the next decade. So far, none of these conditions exist.

The picture in terms of supply/demand gets still more complicated as in Poland the number of vacancies in the private sector is fully flexible and depends only on institutions themselves; and there are no national competitions for places in either public or private institutions. While the number of vacancies in the public sector is strictly regulated by the Ministry (as those places are subsidized by the state), the private sector in general enrolls all those wishing to study, provided they fulfill the basic formal requirement (except for a few selective top institutions where meeting some academic entry requirements is required). Already in the medium-quality range of both public and private sector institutions, vacancies in many study areas are offered, even at most prestigious public institutions.

Turning toward the Market: Cost-Sharing and Privatization

We will focus now on cost-sharing and (internal and external) privatization. Higher education in several new EU countries, Poland (as well as Romania and Bulgaria) included, has been consistently turning toward privatization, both external (a new booming private sector) and internal (fee-paying courses offered in the nominally free public sector) (Kwiek, 2007). In general terms, privatization is "the transfer of activities, assets and responsibilities from government/public institutions to private individuals and agencies. Education can be privatized if students enroll at private schools or if [higher education] is privately funded" (Belfield and Levin, 2002: 19; Kwiek, 2006). Poland provides examples of both.

The emergence of powerful market mechanisms in public higher education (fee-based teaching for part-time students) and the arrival of the private sector can be viewed as the two different faces of the same process. In existing literature, Polish higher education has generally been discussed in a highly dichotomous manner: either public institutions, or private institutions, or both as opposite to each other. The radical distinctiveness of the public sector from the private sector has been a constant point of reference in both research and policy analyses. But, surprisingly, both sectors can also be looked at as following the same road of privatization if the phenomenon of privatization as applied to higher education is taken more widely. As Daniel C. Levy stressed, "institutions called private and public are not always behaviorally private and public, respectively" (Levy, 1986: 15); and this is indeed the Polish case.

The role of fees in the creeping marketization of Polish higher education is critical. As they are charged by the whole private sector and by part-time study offer of the public sector to 60 percent of all Polish students, the evolution of their levels in both sectors and their future in the public sector is highly relevant. Marketization and privatization meant increasing competition and access. Further marketization, for example, the introduction of fees for all in the public sector, with grants and loans schemes, might mean more competition and substantially more equity as today, after 20 years of volatile transformations, the best and most lucrative places in the public sector are still disproportionately allocated to students from the middle classes. In the last decade, the share of tuition fees from part-time students in the revenues of public institutions was high and varied substantially, depending on the type of institution. Without this particular form of privatization—increasing reliance on fees from part-time students—the Polish public sector would have found it enormously difficult to survive economically. Educational expansion would have been left entirely to the growing private sector which would not have been able to meet unexpectedly high student demand. In the last 10 years, public institutions have become less and less reliant on state subsidies, the share of such subsidies in their income decreasing in the universities from 71 to 66 percent.

From the very beginning, the most important dimension of internal privatization of the public sector was financial: additional revenues for both faculty and for the university. Fees from part-time students were a substantial contribution to university revenues and were much more than merely recovering costs. The revenues were divided between institutions and faculty; for academics, working with part-time students in the public sector meant additional revenues, paid by hours worked. In an initially surprising manner, public institutions in the first half of the 1990s started having two sorts of students (fee-paying and non-fee-paying, the former academically weaker), two sorts of curricula (academically weaker for the fee-paying students), and two different teaching times (weekdays for non-fee-paying students and weekends for fee-paying students). Those with higher cultural and human capital studied as non-fee-paying full-time students, those with lower cultural and human capital studied as fee-paying, part-time students. The numerical expansion opened the system to new segments of society but these newcomers have been attending mostly the two academically inferior forms of studies: those offered in the private sector and those offered for fee-paying weekend students in the public sector.

Tuition fees have therefore played a critical role in the expansion of both the private and public sectors (Kwiek, 2009b). In 2006, total funds collected through fees reached approx. 1.2 billion Euros, with only a slightly higher share going to private institutions (approx. 610 million Euros): 50:50 percent. Thus, in practice, almost half of all higher education fees went to the public sector which is nominally "free". This is the most striking financial aspect of the privatization of the public sector.

In the last decade, the share of the total income from all fees charged in Poland (regarded as 100 percent) steadily increased for the private sector, from 38.4 percent in 1997 to 52.3 percent in 2007. It was only in 2006 that the share of the total income from fees for the private sector was bigger than 50 percent. At the same time, the share of the total income from fees collected by public institutions was decreasing steadily, from 61.6 percent in 1997 to 47.7 percent in 2007. In financial terms, the public sector (fee-paying part-time mode of teaching only) was steadily losing to the private sector (fully fee-based and financially self-reliant).

There is limited price competition between public institutions as full-time studies in all of them are free, and revenue-driven part-time studies do not differentiate themselves by price. There is significant price competition between public and private sectors in the areas where public sector institutions offer fee-based part-time studies, and between private sector institutions themselves. Public institutions are often emulating successful private educational offers,

—— (2009c) Academic entrepreneurship vs. Changing governance and institutional management structures at European universities. *Policy Futures in Education*, 6(6): 757–70.

Levy, D. C. (1986) *Higher Education and the State in Latin America. Private Challenges to Public Dominance.* Chicago: University of Chicago Press.

—— (2007) Legitimacy and privateness: Central and Eastern European Higher Education in a global context. In Slantcheva, S. & Levy, D. C. (Eds) *Private HE in Post-Communist Europe: In Search of Legitimacy.* New York: Palgrave.

Leyden, D. P. (2005) *Adequacy, Accountability, and the Future of Public Education Funding.* Dordrecht: Springer.

Machin, S. and Mcnally, S. (2007) *Tertiary Education Systems and Labour Markets.* Paris: OECD.

Ministry of Science and Higher Education (MoSHE). (2009) *Assumptions of the New Draft Law on Higher Education.* Warsaw: MoSHE. Available from: http://www.bip.nauka.gov.pl/_gAllery/73/10/7310/20091030_EEE_zalozenia_po_RM.pdf

Organisation for Economic Cooperation and Development (OECD). (2004) *On the Edge: Securing a Sustainable Future for Higher Education.* Paris: OECD.

—— (2006) *OECD Economic Surveys. Poland.* Paris: OECD.

—— (2007) *OECD Reviews of Tertiary Education. Poland.* Paris: OECD.

—— (2008) *Tertiary Education for the Knowledge Society. Vol. 1.* By P. Santiago, K. Tremblay, E. Basri and E. Arnal. Paris: OECD.

Schwarzenberger, A. (2008) *Public/Private Funding of Higher Education: A Social Balance.* Hannover: HIS.

Shattock, M. (2005) European universities for entrepreneurship. *Higher Education Management and Policy,* 17(3): 1–16.

United Nations Development Programme (UNDP) (2007) *Edukacja dla pracy: Raport o rozwoju spolecznym Polska 2007.* Warszawa: United Nations Development Programme (UNDP). (In Polish.)

Williams, G. (Ed.). (2003) *The Enterprising University: Reform, Excellence, and Equity.* Buckingham, England: SRHE (Society for Research in Higher Education) and Open University Press.

12
The Marketization of Higher Education
A Perspective from Japan

FUTAO HUANG

Student Education

Numbers of Institutions by Type and Sector

Contemporary Japanese higher education basically consists of three major types of institution: universities, junior colleges (*Tanki Daigaku* in Japanese) and colleges of technology. In some cases, specialized training colleges (*Sensyuu Gakkou*) are also considered as part of higher education. Students officially enrolled in the Open University of Japan (changed from the University of Air in October 2007) and those pursuing their higher education learning through TV or radio in other regular universities and junior colleges are also included in the data.

Prior to 1 April 2004, when all national universities became national university corporations, there had been three sectors of higher education institutions: national, public and private. They were founded by the central government, local public authorities and educational foundations respectively. Since 2004, with a further deregulation of the "Standards for Establishment of Universities" and new reforms on the establishment of higher education institutions, a totally new sector of universities has emerged: institutions founded by a company or a corporation. By 2008, seven such universities had been approved by the Ministry of Education, Cultures, Sports, Science and Technology (MEXT). For example, Tokyo University of Career Development which was founded by Tokyo Legal Mind K.K. Company in 2004, Digital Hollywood University by Digital Hollywood Co., Ltd in 2005, and Cyber University by Japan Cyber Educational Institute, Ltd in 2007 are now well-known. However, because of difficulties in attracting sufficient students, undertaking activities that violate government regulations, and other troubles, some of these universities have either stopped recruiting or have been changed to private universities.

According to the School Education Law, "the university, as a center of learning, shall aim at teaching and studying deeply professional learning and technical arts as well as providing a broad knowledge and developing the intellectual, moral and practical abilities" (Article 52) (MONBUSHO, 1989). Normally, graduates from senior higher school or those who have completed 12 years of schooling are qualified to apply for admission. In universities, both undergraduate courses leading to Bachelor's degrees and graduate courses leading to Master's and doctoral degrees are provided. At undergraduate level, the normal duration of study is four years, except for faculties of medicine and dentistry which range to six. Graduate education consists of Master's level study and doctoral education. The typical length of study is two years for Master's degrees and three years for PhDs or doctoral degrees.

The two-year junior colleges were initially founded as finishing schools for women being awarded terminal degrees. They are expected "to conduct teaching and research in depth in specialized academic subjects and to cultivate such abilities as are required in vocations or practical life" (Article 69–2, paragraph 1) (MONBUSHO, 1989). Prior to 2005, graduates from junior colleges received the degree of Associate, which is practically equivalent to the "Foundation degree" in the UK and "Associate" in the USA. Since October 2005, a new degree called "Tanki daigakushi" in Japanese, meaning an academic degree awarded by junior colleges in English, has replaced the old "associate".

Colleges of technology have lower entrance standards, primarily providing five-year vocational educational programs for graduates from junior higher schools. "A college of technology shall aim to teach specialized academic subjects in depth and to cultivate the abilities required for certain vocations" (Article 70–72) (ibid.). The Sensyuu Gakkou (special training school) "conducts systematic education to develop the abilities necessary for certain vocations or practical life, or to enhance cultural standards" (Article 82–2) (ibid.). Courses cover at least one year but many of them are for two years or more.

In 2007, leaving aside the special training schools, there were 1,254 higher education institutions. By type, there are 756 universities, 434 junior colleges and 64 colleges of technology. The private sector has 78.2 percent of the total. Regarding types of institutions by sector, in contrast to the high percentage role of the national sector among colleges of technology (85.9 percent), the private sector accounts for the biggest share of the number of institutions, with 91.7 percent of the junior colleges and 76.7 percent of the universities (MEXT, 2008a).

Number of Students by Type and Sector

In 2007, there were 3,165,775 students in total, including 262,113 at graduate level, 2,716,134 at undergraduate level in universities, junior colleges and colleges of technology, and 187,528 in correspondence schools. The private sector constituted 75.7 percent of the total, the national sector had 19.9 percent. In terms of levels, the private sector had 77.3 percent of university undergraduates, the national sector had 58.7 percent of graduates (MEXT, 2008a).

According to government statistics, 36.3 percent of students at undergraduate level were studying social sciences, 16.7 percent engineering and 15.8 percent humanities. However, it should be noted that the percentage of students by discipline even at the same level varied greatly according to different sectors, especially between the national and private sectors. For example, the share of enrollments in the national sector comprises 30.6 percent in engineering and 15.7 percent in education and teacher training. In contrast, in the private sector, enrollments are concentrated in social sciences and humanities. At junior college level 29.8 percent of students were in education, 20.8 percent in home economics and 12.4 percent in humanities. The total gender rate of 179,958 students in junior colleges is: 20,647 male and 159,311 female students (MEXT, 2008a).

The role played by the private sector in achieving mass and universal access to higher education in Japan cannot be overstated. As early as 1963, when enrollments in Japan's higher education system had reached 15.4 percent of the school leaver age group, private institutions enrolled 67 percent of this group. By the 1970s, the figures for private universities and private junior colleges, and private students enrolled in these two types of institutions, had all surpassed 70 percent (RIHE, 2004). Compared with many countries in North America and Europe, as well as plenty in Asia, one of the most striking characteristics of Japan's higher education is that the private sector makes up the largest proportion of the total at university and junior college levels.

The rate of student enrollments in higher education institutions varies substantially depending on which institutions are included in the calculation. As of 2008, student enrollments in postsecondary education institutions reached 78 percent of the 18-year-age population, with 56.2 percent of students at universities, junior colleges or colleges of technology (fourth year), and the remainder at correspondence schools, the Open University of Japan (regular courses) and specialized training schools (specialized or vocational courses) (MEXT, 2009a).

Funding

Among national, public and private sectors, significant differences exist not only in roles, functions and student composition, but also in the allocation of public funding, including research grants.

Public funding for national universities, or national university corporations since 2004, varies significantly according to their size, missions, functions and character; over half of their annual revenue comes directly from the government. By the end of the 1990s the government share of national university revenue was 66 percent. Tuition fees provided for 11.7 percent of university revenue and the income of hospitals affiliated to individual universities provided for 19.1 percent. The rest of the revenue comes from other sources (CNUFM, 2001).

Although all national universities have become national university corporations, a change which triggered a continuous drop in the public funding of national and public sectors after 2004, in 2006 on a national average basis the share of public funding in total revenue, including operating budget, normal research grants for all faculties, and subsidies for infrastructures and equipment, was still more than 40 percent, with less than 15 percent of revenue in the form of tuition fees charged to students (CNUFM, 2007). In contrast, public funding was only 12.3 percent of revenue in private institutions in 2005, with tuition fees 60 percent of the total. The financing of Japan's private universities relies heavily on tuition fees (SBMIACJ, 2009).

The incorporation of national universities in 2004, followed by a similar incorporation of public universities, has resulted in considerable changes in the financial structure of Japan's higher education. On the one hand, there has been a steady drop in the amount of government expenditure in both national and public sectors, while individual national and public university corporations have been given more freedom to charge tuition and fees according the their chosen level. On the other hand, government has increased the amount of competitive funding, including both research project grants and special budgets for a variety of projects or programs related to educational activities (Jibu et al., 2008).

The proportion of Japan's GDP devoted to expenditure in higher education is much lower than many other OECD countries. On a comparative basis, students and their parents contribute a high share of educational expenses.

Regulation

Prior to 1991, the document "Standards for establishment of universities", which is stipulated and imposed by the central government, played a vital role in accrediting and regulating all sectors of higher education. There are numerous articles in the "Standards", but they can be divided into two parts. One concerns the design of the university curriculum, including the classification, structure and sequence of educational programs, as well as minimum units, distribution of total units and the ratio of each subject to the units required for graduation. The other deals with infrastructure and facilities. These criteria are laid down as a benchmark for the accreditation of any new universities and to assure the quality of all Japan's higher education institutions in advance.

With deregulation of the "Standards" since the early 1990s, especially since 2004, national university corporations not only have more freedom to design and implement curricula according to their own missions, goals and objectives, but are also allowed to manage themselves as corporations by introducing market mechanisms. At the same time, the central government has urged institutions to conduct self-monitoring and self-evaluation to make their teaching and research activities, and their management, more accountable and to assure their educational quality. The School Education Law, amended in 2002, makes it compulsory for all universities, junior colleges, colleges of technology and law schools to be evaluated by a quality assurance agency accredited by MEXT. The overall conditions of teaching, research, organizational management, and facilities and equipment of universities, junior colleges and colleges of technology must be evaluated at least once every seven years. The overall conditions of the curricula, faculties and other education activities of professional graduate schools (such as law schools) must be evaluated at least once every five years.

The incorporation of national universities has constituted a major change in the regulatory structure of Japan's higher education system. One apparent outcome is that all national universities are no longer directly subject to government. The central government still assumes strong responsibility for accreditation and for closing an institution and it is also responsible for providing the necessary revenue for each individual national university corporation. However, the budgeted allocation from the central government is now based on an evaluation. The government takes more account of *ex post facto* evaluation and places less emphasis on advance regulation than previously (Huang, 2006a). This is a very significant shift.

In relation to internal governance in the national university corporations, more powers have been given to governing bodies at institutional level and there has been a reduction in the autonomous rights residing in faculty meetings. Instead of the sole deliberative council that existed in individual national universities prior to April 2004, the governing bodies at institutional level now comprise a Board of Directors, an Education and Research Council and an Administrative Council. The President of each university corporation becomes the chief executive and carries the strongest powers. In addition, while the Education and Research Board is comprised of internal representatives and has the main responsibility for important educational and research activities, the Board of Directors and the Administrative Council are open to participation by non-university external experts who are expected to be involved in internal governance and management. The aim is to ensure that each university corporation is responsive to the needs of society, and to promote cooperation with industry. Consequently, the traditional pattern of governance in the Japanese national universities has been fundamentally changed. There are reduced autonomous rights and powers at faculty level, and the power of the bureaucracy within each university has been expanded well beyond that of academic staff. In particular, leadership from the top by the President has become greatly emphasized (Huang, 2006b).

Two notable independent organizations are involved with carrying out professional accreditation activities. One is the Japan Accreditation Board for Engineering Education (JABEE), which was founded in 1999. In collaboration with the academic community and with industry, the JABEE examines and accredits engineering education programs, assisted by appropriate discipline-specific committees from its member societies and from the JABEE itself. It is mainly concerned with conducting quality assurance and improvement of engineering education in the light of internationally standardized criteria. The other is the Japan Law Foundation which was approved by the MEXT in 2004 as a third-party evaluation agency to exercise professional accreditation in law schools. In addition to these key organizations, the Japan University Accreditation Association (JUAA), which is independent of government and modeled on the American system, accredits higher education institutions that had previously gained government recognition for specific programs or for specified fields of study on a voluntary basis.

With respect to market entry conditions, with the steady drop in numbers in the 18-year-age group in recent years, and the increasing participation in the market by both national and public university corporations, it has become increasingly difficult for many small and local private institutions, and even for a few public and national institutions, to recruit sufficient entrants. It is estimated that in 2008 alone, nearly half of all private institutions had difficulty meeting their student quotas. This is expected to continue. Hence, in contrast with the national and public sectors, private institutions have been making great efforts to explore more diversified and flexible ways of attracting students.

The vast majority of national and public institutions maintain their traditional way of recruiting students through student achievement in the unified examination organized by the National Center for University Entrance Examinations on fixed dates. But private institutions recruit new entrants all year around. They provide more information to potential applicants and, especially, more opportunities to enter. Private institutions usually start their recruiting activities as early as May, only one month after the beginning of the new academic year. In some institutions, such activities last till March of the following year, one month prior to the next academic year, constituting a 10-month recruitment season. In addition to the unified examination, and as for national and public institutions, private institutions have begun to draw an increasing number of new entrants through interviews with applicants, assessment of applicants' reports, recommendation letters by senior higher schools, and even self-recommendation documents by applicants themselves. Entry conditions in private institutions are more affected by market forces than is the case in the national and public sectors. This creates risks and uncertainty in the operation of private institutions.

The major disciplines represented in Japan's higher education and research systems are literature, education, law, economics, sociology, sciences, engineering, agriculture, veterinary medicine, medicine, dentistry, pharmacy, home economy, fine arts, music, physical education and health science. Except for a very small number of private institutions and local national or public universities, the vast majority of four-year universities are qualified to provide a wide range of various subjects or programs at different levels based on the disciplines discussed earlier in this paragraph. As mentioned earlier, the large number of private universities tends to provide more practical and applied educational programs, typically market-oriented, especially in social sciences and humanities.

Prior to the 1990s there had been only two types of academic degrees: Master's and PhDs. Since 2001, both Bachelor degrees and professional degrees at a graduate level have been added into the nation's academic system. Over the last decade, there has been a rapid growth in numbers of all four types. There is no official regulatory document that defines the specific types of either academic degrees or professional degrees which should be awarded at an institutional level (NIADUE, 2005).

Academic Research and Scholarship

Size of Market, Government Policies and Major Research Areas

The definition of a researcher varies widely according to country. In Japan, the term "researcher" not only includes faculty members, PhD students, and staff in medicine at universities and colleges, but also includes staff with Bachelor students who carry out research activities with a specific research topic (MEXT, 2007).

In 2007, the total number of researchers in Japan was approximately 830,000, an increase of 0.1 percent from 2006 (SBMIACJ, 2008). Researchers in Japan mainly come from four sectors: government or public organizations (4.0 percent), higher education institutions (36.6 percent), business enterprises (58.5 percent), and non-profit institutions (1.0 percent) (SBMIACJ, 2008). In 2008, there were 22,370 institutions in the business enterprise sector that carried out research, with 483,728 researchers. There were 1,040 research institutions classified as public or non-profit organizations, with 41,071 researchers; and 3,498 research institutions at universities and colleges with 302,493 researchers (MEXT, 2008a).

There has been a gradual growth in total numbers of researchers. The number of researchers in the business enterprise sector has expanded the most rapidly, from less than 300,000 persons in 2000 to nearly 490,000 persons in 2008, and contributing enormously to the overall growth. In contrast, there has been no radical increase in the number of researchers at universities and colleges.

Funding, Evaluation and Training of Researchers

The character of research activity in Japan is also reflected in the proportion of R&D expenditure by research sector and type of activity. Figure 12.1 shows that at the national level, over 60 percent of expenditure is provided for experimental development research, particularly in the business enterprise sector, with over 70 percent of expenditure on development research. In contrast, only 13.8 percent of total expenditure is provided for basic research at the national level.

- The shape (structure, governance, composition) of the system;
- The evaluation and funding of research;
- The funding of student education;
- The quality assurance of teaching;
- The relationship between research and teaching.[1]

Before coming to these, a number of comments may be appropriate:

- A wide coverage of policy areas is needed if all aspects of a system are to be healthy;
- Because of the ground to be covered, and the constraints of space, the discussion is necessarily a somewhat summary one;
- UK experience and practice plays a major part in the discussion. This is partly because this is the system with which the author is most familiar, but also because the UK occupies an instructive "middle position" between the more marketized systems (the US, Australia) and the less marketized ones (the Nordics, most of continental Europe);
- No distinction is made in the relative scale of systems. Bleiklie (2003: 346; 2007: 396) suggests that overall state "steering" is possible at the national level only in relatively small systems, whereas integration takes place at the regional (or even local) level in larger ones. This is in fact the approach that will be adopted when we come to consider system diversity. Similarly, no account is taken of different state constitutions or cultures;
- Taken as a whole, the policies proposed may strike some observers as idealistic, even Panglossian. But nothing is put forward that is not technically feasible, and in nearly every case examples are given of where these policies are already being applied in some measure;
- It is recognized that a major role is foreseen for the state, with attendant risks of excessive "bureaucracy". However it is the central argument of the book that by themselves market forces will not produce an effective, efficient or fair higher education system which produces the full range of public and private goods in a cost-effective manner. If we want such a system, there is no alternative to state action through regulation and financial support for institutions and students, combined with a large measure of institutional autonomy and self-regulation (Steier, 2003; Newman et al., 2004).

The Shape of the System

The starting point therefore is the need for the state to determine the overall aims and shape of the system. The main issues include:

- The purposes of the system;
- The entry rules;
- The balance between "public" and "private" provision;
- Institutional status and autonomy;
- The institutional division of labor;
- How to achieve some measure of system integration.

The Purposes of the System

A number of writers (e.g., Zemsky et al., 2005) call for a renewed discussion of the purposes of higher education and the extent and ways in which these are realized through public and private means. A famous statement of the purposes of higher education was that of the UK Robbins Committee:

- Instruction in skills suitable to play a part in the general division of labour;
- What is taught should be taught in such a way as to promote the general powers of the mind;
- Advancement of learning;
- The transmission of a common culture and common standards of citizenship (Committee on Higher Education, 1963: paragraphs 25–28).

Amongst more recent formulations is that of the US Futures Project:

- Bearing responsibility for student learning;
- Providing for social mobility by moving beyond access to attainment;
- Protecting the public investment by addressing efficiency and productivity;
- Supporting elementary and secondary education;
- Conducting needed research;
- Serving as society's critic;
- Building civic engagement to sustain the democracy (Newman et al., 2004: 220).

These are merely examples. The point is the need for some authoritative, generally accepted, statement of the main purposes of the system: it may seem idealistic but without it, there can be no secure way of determining the value of any particular policy or policy change that may be advocated.

Market Entry

Most systems have means of determining which institutions should offer higher education. In the UK, distinctions are made between the power to award taught degrees (including Master's Degrees), research degrees (including PhDs) and university title. The criteria are laid down by the government and involve both academic maturity and financial viability. Advice is given by the national quality agency using a peer review process but the decisions are made by ministers. Once the powers have been acquired it is very difficult to lose them although privately owned degree awarding institutions have to re-submit themselves for further scrutiny every six years. In America, an institution requires accreditation by one of the regional accrediting commissions if its students are to benefit from Federal financial support. Accreditation can be withdrawn, or conditions be laid down for continuing accreditation.

It is suggested here that, because of the importance of credentials in a modern, knowledge-based society, the state should control market participation, with entry regulated through public rules and procedures, and that continuing involvement should be subject to some form of periodic institutional accreditation (see later, "Quality Assurance").

Private or Public?

Private institutions play a major role in a number of systems (Chile, Korea, Japan, the US, Poland, Portugal), and in many others their role is growing though still modest. But what exactly is a "private" higher education institution? There are two key dimensions, ownership and funding.

In a recent survey, Vincent-Lancrin refers to the definitions used in international statistics:

A **public** *institution is controlled and managed directly by a public education authority or agency, or is controlled and managed either by a government agency directly or by a governing body (Council, Committee etc.), most of whose members are appointed by a public authority or elected by public franchise.*

A **private** *institution is controlled and managed by a non-governmental organization (e.g., a church, trade union or business enterprise), or its Governing Board consists mainly of members not selected by a public government agency but by private institutions* (Vincent-Lancrin, 2009: 124, original author's emphasis).

He goes on to distinguish between private institutions that are more than 50 percent reliant on government funding ("government-dependent" institutions) and those that are not ("independent" private institutions). However, even a much lower level of reliance on public funding creates some dependence such that the institution would be in serious difficulty, at least in the short to medium term, if the funding were suddenly to be withdrawn. This is the position of the leading Ivy League institutions in the United States and Oxford and Cambridge in Britain. Moreover, even private institutions that receive no direct state funding often receive indirect funding through tax breaks and other devices (as well as Federal aid, students of private institutions are eligible for State aid in most US States: Eckstein, 2009). At the same time, of course, "public" institutions are raising increasing amounts of revenue from private sources, particularly in Korea, Japan, the US, Australia, Canada and New Zealand. In other words, whether one is talking about ownership or funding, the public/private distinction appears increasingly irrelevant. Should we therefore abandon it? There are at least two reasons why it is worth retaining it.

The first concerns accountability. In the last resort, public institutions are answerable to some public entity that is by definition publicly accountable. They operate within a regulated public sector that demands certain tasks in return for its financial support. This is not the case with private ones. Ehrenberg (2002: 23–26) indeed argues that, just because they do not have to account to state legislatures or executives, the major American private institutions are under much less pressure than the public ones to restrain their spending and costs (as we saw in Chapter 3, the relative freedom of the leading private institutions to charge "what the market will bear" is a major reason for the huge rise in tuition fees across America in the past 20 years).

The second concerns those private institutions that are established with the purpose of making a financial return for their owners. Whilst they may well be meeting a market need that conventional public institutions are not, and even though in practice their day to day activities may not be so very different from those of "not for profit" ones, there is always the danger that they will skim off the more remunerative areas of the market, in turn reducing the ability of "not for profit" institutions to cross-subsidize less attractive programs, and ultimately putting at risk that provision and (ironically) the degree of choice that it represents for consumers (Duderstadt and Womack, 2003; Newman et al., 2004; Zemsky et al., 2005).

In a comprehensive survey, Teixeira and Amaral (2001: 390–91) conclude that whilst they may meet market needs that public institutions do not, the private sector is mostly characterized by low-risk behavior, and a concentration on low-cost and/or safer initiatives. A privatized system cannot offer the range of subjects and programs, let alone the amount, range and quality of research, that a publicly funded one can, which is exactly what the economic theory summarized in Chapter 2 would predict.[2]

What this suggests is that the state needs to have policies and means not only for regulating the activities of private, particularly "for profit", universities and colleges, but also for reviewing periodically their contribution to a healthy system. In particular, private institutions should be required to show that they contribute public benefits proportional to the financial benefits they receive from the public (for a similar view, see Zumeta, 2005). The US Congress in 2008 was considering legislation that would require universities to spend at least 5 percent of their endowments each year, bringing them into line with other non-profit foundations. In the UK, the Charities Commission has just required two "public" (i.e., independent, private) schools to increase their spending on free places or risk losing their charitable status.

Status and Autonomy

How much autonomy should higher education institutions enjoy? This has several aspects, but the central question is how far institutions are constrained in the key choices they make about their mission and field(s) of operation, the subjects and programs to be offered, the kinds of research to be pursued, the employment and remuneration of staff, procurement, etc. through some form of state control.

At one extreme, the "for profit" private institutions in the US may choose to submit to periodic institutional (and professional) accreditation but are otherwise subject only to the same regulation as other commercial entities. At the other extreme, universities in some continental European countries were until relatively recently subject to close state control over their programs and awards (e.g., in The Netherlands universities are still required to get government approval if they wish to enter a new field of study). However, as we saw in some of the system case studies, there is now a program of liberalization aimed at moving these institutions closer to the public institutions in America and Britain (Enders and Musselin, 2007: 10). This reflects the belief, which is generally supported by the research evidence, that institutions will be more effective, and efficient, when they have a considerable degree of control over their destiny. But what happens when this autonomy leads to lots of institutions making similar choices? This takes us to the central question of how system diversity is to be secured.

The Institutional Division of Labor

There are basically two questions here:

- Should there be some diversity of provision?
- What should it be and how should it be created and sustained?

The argument for diversity rests on the notion that as higher education expands in scale and in the number and variety of functions it fulfils, it is increasingly difficult (as well as expensive) for a single form of provision to meet all the demands being placed on it. There may also be an issue, going back to the earlier discussion of academic and vocational drift, of whether, without some measure of state supervision, universities, and particularly many faculty, would wish to differentiate themselves as much as might be societally desirable.

This leads to the argument that marketization is the best means of securing diversity and, indeed, that marketization is the best way of countering those forces within the academy to which we have just referred (e.g., Geiger, 1996). This argument is rejected, on the basis (which will by now be tediously familiar) that higher education markets do not operate like conventional ones, where consumer choice between search goods may produce a wide range of products. Whilst some degree of competition between institutions is certainly desirable, unrestrained competition seems very unlikely to produce a genuinely diverse system. There is in fact no alternative to state action if market and non-market pressures are to be reconciled (for an argument on similar lines, see Kyvik, 2004: 406–7). The issue then is what form that diversity should take.

There is an argument that it is program diversity that matters, and especially diversity in the number and range of qualifications at different levels in different disciplines. However, this often translates into institutional diversity, with the curriculum varying between institutions with different missions even where the subject and qualification is apparently similar (Teichler, 2008: 353). It is diversity at institutional level which is seen here as the key to diversity of provision. But what is the best means of achieving this?

In Europe and Australia, the answer historically has been through the creation of separate sectors of "non-university" institutions (polytechnics, Fachhochschulen, Instituts Universitaires de Technologie, colleges of advanced education, regional colleges, etc.). These have usually been prevented from offering research degrees or receiving state funding for research, though they may have received funding from local or regional authorities or agencies. The main problem is maintaining the distinctiveness of the sector over time due not least to the ambitions of academic communities in the "inferior" institutions (Scott, 1995; Teichler, 2007; Horta et al., 2008). In the US, the almost uniquely diverse character of the system has historically been due to a number of factors. Eckel (2008: 178) refers to the Jeffersonian ideals of limited government and full freedom of expression, plurality of funding sources, and the commitment to opportunity and social mobility; he also notes the erosion of diversity as marketization has intensified.

One mechanism which appears to have achieved some balance between these various forces has been the creation in a number of US States of systems where the State government, or a body acting on its behalf, lays down boundaries that constrain institutional development by assigning missions to individual institutions. California, Texas and Wisconsin are amongst the best known examples. In this way, each type of institution supports the other: the leading institutions remain subject to some degree of public control whilst the less prestigious institutions benefit from association with their peers. There may also be economic advantages through the sharing of academic programs and/or administrative functions. Depending on geography, it may be that something along these lines (a division of labor that operates at sub-system level) is a better solution to the problem of sustaining diversity than the designation of separate sectors on the European/Australian model or the attempt to combine different missions within one institution, where one form of higher education almost invariably trumps the others. The main drawback is that such a system interposes an additional level of governance (and possibly unnecessary bureaucracy) between the individual institution and the funding authority. Whichever system is adopted, there needs to be a process whereby students are able to transfer between institutions. This implies the need for articulation agreements between institutions so that barriers to movement can be minimized (Moodie, 2002). There is also a case for greater transparency about institutional missions and characteristics (Eckel, 2008; van Vught, 2008), provided these are not confused with relative educational quality.

Means of State Action

The issue here is how the public interest in a healthy system is to be secured. What specific functions will need to be discharged if a balance is to be found between public and private interests? How is an accommodation to be reached between the interests of one institution (or group of institutions) and the system as a whole, where this is felt to be necessary or desirable? The short answer(s) would appear to be regulation and development. We shall deal with regulation when we come to quality assurance. The focus here is on system development.

We are imagining a situation where there is increasing competition between institutions for students and research funding, and where the problems with consumer information have still to be resolved. We are also talking about a situation where the homogenizing forces within the academy remain strong. How then can we create and maintain a diverse, responsive and efficient system?

The suggestion is made that each higher education system should have a "development agency" with a legal duty to secure, by every means in its power, a diverse, accessible, efficient and high-quality system. The precise title, terms of reference and status will naturally vary between countries, as well as the relationship to government (in some countries it could be an arm of the central ministry, in others it might be an "arms length" agency). The main functions would be:

- To periodically (every 5–10 years) review and report on the structure and operation of the system so as to establish how near or far it might be from the desired model;
- To take, or advise others to take, correcting actions.

Within the first of these there would be a specific duty to keep under review the numbers, quality and health of the higher education workforce, reflecting the importance of this for a healthy higher education system (see later, "Conclusions").

The correcting actions might concern the status and role of individual institutions or groups of institutions (the ultimate power to determine these would remain with government or the highest state authority). But the main means would be through the funding of individual institutions on the basis of institutional development plans (see later, "The Funding of Student Education"). This would be a means of promoting or protecting particular kinds of provision, including specific subjects, activities and types of institution. The agency would also be involved, together with the relevant institutional authorities, in institutional restructuring.

The Evaluation and Funding of Research

> Research became the coin of the realm, the best way to get one's ticket punched for institutions and professors alike.
>
> (Massy, 2003: 19)

The discussion continues with the evaluation and funding of research because it is this—in systems where academic staff conduct research alongside teaching and other activities—which largely differentiates institutions. Indeed, Horta et al. (2008) argue that it is *only* through the differential funding of research that a genuinely diverse system can be created. Bearing this in mind, the questions that need to be considered include:

- Should research be done in universities?
- Should university research receive public funding?
- On what basis should such funding be allocated?
- What are the benefits and detriments of competitive research funding?
- How should any unanticipated consequences be dealt with?
- How should the impacts of commercially funded university research be controlled?

Should Research Be Carried Out in Universities?

Historically, higher education systems can be broadly divided into those where research was conducted in universities and those where it was not, also bearing in mind the fact that, even where it is conducted alongside teaching, research is a relatively recent arrival: it is only since the Second World War that it has been a major driver of university activity, and even now a substantial proportion of research in certain disciplines is conducted away from the academy even in countries with a substantial university research effort (Ben-David, 1977).

Nevertheless, the number of systems where academic research is conducted outside universities appears to be dwindling (mainly in the former Soviet bloc although in France, Germany and one or two other West European countries substantial amounts of academic research are still conducted in separate research institutes, albeit often by existing university faculty). For present purposes, it will be assumed that research is conducted in universities, and that it represents a significant part of the responsibilities and activities of mainstream faculty. We will consider the corollary—what should be the relationship between research and other academic activities, especially teaching—later.

Should University Research Receive Public Funding?

When we reviewed in Chapter 2 the argument for non-market coordination, we noted that research was a classic case where the market left to itself would produce sub-optimal quantities (and probably quality) of research. This would be societally disadvantageous because it would mean that the volume and quality of the public goods stemming from the enlargement and application of knowledge would be inferior. In fact, an increasing amount of university research in countries like America and Britain *is* commercially funded but it tends not to be "basic" or "discovery" ("blue skies") research. So even in the US, Federal and State funding plays a crucial part in supporting academic research, though it should also be borne in mind that (as also in Britain and elsewhere) the bulk of financial support for academic research comes from institutions' own resources including, in many cases, resources obtained for other purposes such as student education. It should also be borne in mind that public funding supports not only the conduct of research by faculty but also the education and training of future researchers (Johnstone and Marcucci, 2007: 30).

What Should Be the Basis of the Funding of University Research?

Just as research is now conducted in universities in most systems, so it is now funded separately from teaching in many cases. Broadly speaking, there are two ways in which public funding for research can be allocated:

- Core funding distributed to all research activities on some formulaic basis;
- Competitive funding distributed to some research activities on the basis of past or future performance (Horta et al., 2008: 152).

Core Funding

By "research activities" we mean the work of faculty and the resources and facilities that are needed to enable them to conduct research: libraries, laboratories, support services, etc. Faculty here importantly includes research and other students—postgraduate and even undergraduate—to the extent that their time and expenses are not funded separately. As mentioned in Chapter 6, under the UK "dual support" system, research infrastructure is funded by the Higher Education Funding Council, whilst research projects are funded by the Research Councils. The latter's grants now include a contribution (80 percent) toward overhead costs.

Competitive Funding

Increasingly, research is funded on a competitive basis ("selectivity"). This is true not only at system level but also within institutions (for recent reviews, see Lucas, 2006; Vincent-Lancrin, 2006; Hicks, 2009; McNay, forthcoming, a and b; Salmi, 2009b). The evaluation can be at the proposal stage or at some later point. It is usually some combination of performance indicators and peer review, with international comparators increasingly in evidence. It can be of an individual researcher, a project, a doctoral program, a research unit or department, an institution, or even several institutions. The focus may be on people, on products (publications, patents), or on both. The funding may be tied to one or several of these levels or there may be discretion on the part of the recipient as to how the money is used (in the case of the UK Research Assessment Exercise [RAE], the money was given to institutions rather than to the departments that were the subject of the evaluation). The amount of money does not need to be huge: Hicks (2009: 400) notes that even a small amount of selective funding can have a significant impact on behavior. It is the assessment, and the impact on reputation, which matters: "nothing less than the positional status of every institution was at stake" (Marginson, 1997: 74).[3]

What Are the Benefits and Detriments of Competitive Funding?

As already noted in Chapter 3, the main benefits of research selectivity appear to lie in the better use of resources, the reduction or restraint of costs, and the elimination or reduction of "poor" research. As Geuna and Martin (2003: 296) say, a performance-based system gives a mechanism to link research to policy, a way to shift priorities across fields, and a rational method of moving resources from less well-performing fields to areas where they can be used to greater effect. The negatives include the transactions costs of making applications (the Higher Education Policy Institute has estimated that the costs of obtaining UK Research Council funds amounts to some 20 percent of the total funds available); the risk that research choices may be skewed, and especially that innovative or cross-disciplinary research will be discounted in favor of more conservative, discipline-based research; and the scope for games playing as institutions focus their resources on trying to work the system rather than improve research quality (Clarke, 2005: 195). Another problem is that, almost inevitably, the evaluations tend to be backward looking, favoring established researchers rather than up and coming ones. There are also wider detriments since competitive research funding leads over time to a growing concentration of research both institutionally (Vincent-Lancrin, 2006: 183; Horta et al., 2008: 154) and geographically (Adams and Smith, 2004). This concentration often covers not only the funding of faculty research but also the funding of research students (Powell and Green, 2006).

If it goes too far, such a concentration has a number of negative consequences:

- It may actually damage research performance. A statistical analysis of the 2008 RAE (Whiteley, 2009) suggests that research performance declines once an institution gets too big (over 10,000 faculty). An analysis of the 1995 US NRC rankings of political science departments (Jackman and Siverson, 1996) found no correlation between faculty size and productivity;
- It may damage research at less "research intensive" institutions. This is an almost inevitable, even if not intended, consequence of selectivity. In the UK, the RAE acted as a signalling device helping the more prestigious institutions to find future research "stars" from less prestigious ones. Selectivity makes it harder for those less research intensive institutions to link faculty research with other activities such as teaching (this was indeed the rationale for the UK Research Informed Teaching Fund—see later, "The Relationship between Research and Teaching"). It is in these institutions that the sharpest tensions between research and teaching often arise as resources are diverted from teaching to support researchers and bolster RAE submissions and Research Council bids whilst other faculty both absorb heavier teaching loads and suffer reduced status as "non-research active";
- Excessive concentration reduces still further the possibility of parity of esteem between different institutional missions;
- Excessive concentration inevitably strengthens the hand of the most prestigious institutions with government and other funders so that system policies are driven by the aspirations and needs of those institutions rather than by those of the system as a whole (as has been seen recently in Britain with opportunistic lobbying by the larger research intensives for still more money to be allocated to scientific research to help with the economic recovery).

It is therefore ironic that, as noted earlier, there appears to be no generally agreed view as to whether competitive funding actually improves the overall quality of research. What does seem to be clear, however, is that whilst some degree of concentration may be inevitable, too much concentration represents a sub-optimal use of public resources for research.

How Should Any Unanticipated Consequences Be Dealt With?

Concluding his survey of selective funding regimes, McNay (forthcoming, a: 17) suggests, as guides to how evaluation should be done: "Use of a hybrid process, clarity of objectives and criteria, transparency of approaches, robust data and, above all, sensitivity to consequences".

Before considering how to get the best balance between these various benefits and detriments, it may be worth emphasizing the importance of unanticipated consequences. This in turn points to the importance of the funding authority being clear and consistent in the purposes for which different forms of evaluation and funding are applied. Perhaps the biggest problem with the RAE was the damage it caused to other academic activities, particularly teaching (McNay, 1999); this has also been the case in other countries where research has been funded selectively (e.g., Willis, 2009). Some of this resulted from the narrow definition of research adopted, which ruled out the production of valuable scholarly artefacts like learning materials and textbooks. But the main issue was the way in which the RAE privileged research over teaching without any compensating benefits for student education. Again, this is something we will take up in our discussion of the relationship between research and teaching. In the meantime, how shall we proceed in relation to the funding of research?

A Suitable Research Regime

One of the fundamental difficulties in devising a suitable regime for the evaluation and funding of research which captures the benefits of competition and concentration but avoids or reduces the detriments is the fact that there is no single, generally agreed, definition of "research" or other inquiry-based activities such as "scholarship", that are carried out with the object of extending knowledge through the generation of new information, insights or understanding. So a regime that is adopted to improve the quantity and quality of one kind of academic inquiry will not necessarily work for another.

The distinction that seems to be the most relevant for funding purposes is between categories of research and inquiry that are relatively expensive to conduct and those that are not. It is not a coincidence that in Britain the origins of the RAE—and indeed the extension of state funding at Oxbridge at the beginning of the twentieth century—lay in the increasingly heavy costs of research in science and technology (Kogan and Hanney, 2000: 93; Evans, 2009: 66). These are subjects where research usually requires a considerable investment in staff and physical facilities, and where effective research often requires a critical mass of researchers working usually in teams. Competitive funding to identify and nurture the strongest centers and teams would seem appropriate for this kind of research, providing that the wider effects are kept under review. But there is not the same argument for concentration elsewhere. Indeed, there is a strong argument that developments in information and communications technology which facilitate collaboration at a distance further reduce the need for concentration at institutional level (Vincent-Lancrin, 2006: 192).

Other cases where competitive funding, at least for a period of time, would seem appropriate are where there is concern to protect research in a subject for strategic reasons (e.g., defence-related research), where a subject is relatively new and it is desired to establish it as a legitimate research area, and/or where there are concerns about the overall quality of research in a particular subject area. These instances aside, it is suggested that research and other forms of academic enquiry meeting the definition just offered should be funded on a basis that is pro rata to the staff effort involved. The quantity and quality of the research produced should be monitored as part of general quality assurance, making appropriate use of peer review and relevant quantitative indicators as desired, always bearing in mind the fact that, as Donovan (2009) recently reminded us, "citation measures are not actual measures of research quality, but are the sum of subjective decisions to cite or not to cite". Ideally, this would form part of an integrated process of institutional and departmental review (see later, "Quality Assurance").[4]

Controlling Commercially Funded Research

In the last 20 years the proportion of academic research that is privately financed has increased (Vincent-Lancrin, 2006: 184). This has led to an extensive literature, virtually all of it American, about the implications for universities (Orr, 1997; Slaughter and Leslie, 1997; Powell and Owen-Smith, 2002; Bok, 2003; Kirp, 2003b; Geiger, 2004b; Newman et al., 2004; Slaughter and Rhoades, 2004; Krimsky, 2005; Washburn, 2005; Calhoun, 2006; Powers, 2006; Greenberg, 2007; Basken, 2009; Scientists for Global Responsibility, 2009).

Private funding has clearly increased the scope, utility and relevance of university research as well as increasing the flow of resources into the academy (albeit that these revenues have tended to be concentrated in certain institutions). But it has also raised issues such as secrecy; falsification, distortion or suppression of results; exchanges of research materials, and conflicts of interest. There are also wider risks to academic standards, to collegiality, to the integrity of the academic community (as we have already seen), and to the standing of the university with the public (Bok, 2003: 106–18).

In terms of remedies, there is a clear division between those who believe that, in view of the value which university scientists attach to their academic standing, such problems will be self-correcting (if there is prior disclosure and transparency) for example, Greenberg (2007) and those who favor stronger action, for example, Krimsky (2005). The latter point out that no one really knows the extent of the potential abuses, noting that nearly all the major cases that have come to light have been as a result of media rather than institutional action, and that, when confronted with these issues, the actions of university authorities have often been feeble.[5]

It is suggested here that the independent regulatory agency proposed for student education (see later) should have the power to investigate and pronounce on privately funded research activities that clearly breach the Mertonian norms of universalism, communalism, disinterestedness and organized scepticism (Krimsky, 2005: 75–79).

The Funding of Student Education

> The challenge . . . is to find new ways to reshape what institutions compete over, how they compete, and the incentives to compete, so that effectiveness and not simply prestige, becomes the prized objective.
>
> (Eckel, 2008: 16)

Whilst there is a considerable literature on the funding of student education, it is relatively rare for any one source to cover all aspects of the matter (one exception is Salmi and Hauptman, 2006). Here, it is assumed that the key issues include:

- Whether to fund teaching through grants to institutions, tuition fees, or some combination of grants and fees;
- The associated conditions, particularly the nature of the fee regime;
- The regime for financing student maintenance (student aid) and the relationship between this and the regime for funding teaching;
- The resultant degree of equity.

The basic assumptions are that (a) the funding of teaching and student aid need to be considered together and (b) whilst the pressures on public expenditure should be accepted, the tuition/aid regime should be governed not only by the competitive financial position of individual institutions or groups of institutions and "what the market will bear", but also by some wider public policy objectives for the effectiveness, efficiency and equity of the system as a whole (Douglass and Keeling, 2008).[6] It should be noted that the discussion refers chiefly to the funding of undergraduate/Baccalaureate/first cycle studies (and indeed to full-time provision where this is separately distinguished). In some systems postgraduate education already has many of the features of a market.

Institutions or Students?

There has over the past 20 years or so been a significant decrease in the proportion of the costs of teaching met from grants to institutions and an increase in the proportion met by tuition fees in nearly all developed systems

As we have already seen, precisely this phenomenon is found in many American universities, and America has of course operated a sort of voucher system since the early 1980s when the Republican-led Congress chose to fund teaching through Federal loan support rather than institutions (Slaughter and Leslie, 1997: 44). (Ironically, given the price leadership role that the leading private institutions have subsequently played, one important driver was the perceived need to restore the market share of the private sector: see Slaughter and Leslie, 1997: 242; cf. Zemsky et al., 2005: 164.) At the same time, the more that teaching is funded through fees, the more it will be seen as a private consumer good and the more students will be likely to adopt a more "instrumental" approach. This is in spite of the fact that (a) the fee typically represents less than half of the cost of tuition (b) both tuition and living costs are very often subsidized and (c) the evidence on returns continues to indicate that higher education is an excellent lifetime investment for most students (McMahon, 2009). There is also a risk that having to pay fees (or repay loans) will skew students toward subjects with a bigger career "payback" (Kezar, 2005). The view that will be taken here is that the costs of tuition should continue to be met through a combination of state grants to institutions and tuition fees, with the proportion represented by fees capped at 45–50 percent.[7]

This is partly on the basis of the wider public benefits, and partly because of the difficulties with consumer information. There are also some specific difficulties with a "pure" voucher system, particularly the challenge which it poses to the stability of institutions' finances (Bekhradnia and Massy, 2009). Vouchers and other demand-driven systems may also be difficult to implement in countries that are part of a regional higher educational agreement unless all the countries concerned adopt the same model (Salmi, 2009a: 109). In any case, many of the benefits which pro-market writers argue from a fee-based system can be obtained through the conditions attached to state funding. It is to this that we now turn.[8]

The Conditions Attached to Grants and Fees

In this section we discuss first the conditions associated with institutional grants and then the various forms of fee regime.

As regards the former, a number of writers have charted the increasing linkage of funding to performance. Salmi (2009a: 98–102) describes a general trend away from negotiated allocations to institutions without any performance criteria toward competition-based mechanisms with performance criteria applying both to institutions and to students. Similarly, Jongbloed (2008: 13–21) sees a trend in state funding away from centralized approaches based on inputs (often based on the previous year's allocation of specific budget items) toward decentralized approaches based on outcomes and performance ("centralized" and "decentralized" here refers to the degree of market orientation: the degree of competition implied by the funding decisions). This increased reliance on market-type coordination mechanisms can also be seen within institutions.

It seems clear that state grants to institutions will increasingly be tied to some sort of performance measurement even as the proportion of state funding diminishes. As Salmi (2009a: 95) notes, the proportion of self-generated income at public tertiary institutions in the OECD nations increased from approximately 20 percent in 1995 to approximately 26 percent 10 years later. In some countries and institutions it was of course much higher. This suggests that we should perhaps be looking more radically at ways in which states (i.e., governments) can ensure that as the share of private financing increases, the public goods traditionally associated with the teaching functions of universities, notably the production of a well-educated workforce, continue to be supplied.

One way in which this could be done is to fund institutions on the basis of their strategic plans (Polytechnics and Colleges Funding Council, 1989; Pratt and Locke, 1994), what has been called "mission-based funding" (Williams and Brown, 2000; Brown, 2001). Institutions would submit their strategic or business plans to the state funding authority, the development agency already proposed. The plans would set out how the institution intended to develop, and would outline the educational, social and economic outcomes proposed for the planning period. The plans would cover: mission, priorities and targets; projected student numbers and subject mix; financial planning, current and capital; prices/costs within the system and the funding authority's indications of the unit of resource; anticipated income; organization, mechanisms and processes including quality assurance; and performance indicators (Pratt and Locke, 1994: 45–46).

The agency would assess these in the light of its own policies, its analysis of societal needs and its commitment to learning and education generally. All of these, together with the criteria being used to assess the plans, would be the subject of prior consultation. The agency would consult the regulatory agency on quality. It would then decide what proportion of each institution's teaching costs to meet. In effect, the agency would be funding the institution's development over a number of years, with the investment "directed to that part of the institution's activities which are strategic, which provide the fundamentals to enable it to prosper in its environment or market and so promise a good return" (Pratt and Locke, 1994: 42).

This approach acknowledges the reality that an increasing proportion of institutional teaching funding is likely to be private; would secure a greater coherence between institutional business plans and the allocation of resources; would sit better with institutions' own business cycles; and above all would provide greater incentives for institutions to concentrate on the activities they are best suited to, rather than conforming to a single, prestige-driven model. It would also enable the public authorities, if they wished, to "steer" institutions and students toward students and activities that may be overlooked in the scramble for status (Rhoades, 2009).

Ideally, plan-based funding would cover all of an institution's core activities, not only teaching but also research, third stream activities (service, knowledge transfer, outreach), and widening participation. It could be introduced gradually, for increasing proportions of state funding (with the remainder continuing to be formulaic, related to student numbers and staff effort). Selective funding approaches such as the RAE could be folded into the process. There would need to be some annual monitoring of student numbers and revenue. The main drawback, as compared with systems where funding is wholly formulaic, is lack of transparency, but that is always an issue where there is a degree of discretion and negotiation. The demands on the institutions and the funding authority would also need careful consideration. It would of course be essential to be sure that institutional provision met basic quality standards (see later, "Quality Assurance").The outcomes would also have to be within the planned minimum (and possibly maximum) levels of funding per student (see later).[9]

Fee Regimes

Marcucci and Johnstone (2007: 303–5) suggest that there are three kinds of fee regime:

- Up front, where the fee is paid at the start of the program by, usually, the student's parents or family. The fee can be targeted or means tested and loans may be available;
- Deferred, where there is the option either of paying up front or where the cost of the fee is met through an income contingent loan or a graduate tax;
- Dual track, where a certain number of free or very low cost university places are awarded by the government based on some criteria, and other places are available to qualified, but lower scoring, students on a tuition fee paying basis or special continuing educational professional courses are set up by universities for which they charge tuition fees.

In any regime, fees can be differentiated by program cost, level, university sector; by the student's domicile; and by whether the student graduates within a set time.

The regime chosen depends in part on who(m) is seen as the main beneficiary. As Marcucci and Johnstone say, deferred regimes have become more popular as a way of reconciling requiring students to contribute to their higher educational costs with their inability to do so whilst still in school. Of the alternatives, a graduate tax is fairer in that (a) it relates the repayments to the level of benefits received rather than to the costs incurred and (b) it is more favorable to students from less favored backgrounds and/or those who pursue less well-remunerated careers such as in the public services. Paying a slightly level higher of income tax on graduation may also be less of a disincentive to enter higher education than a long period of debt.

Student Aid

> Federal programs and policies that used market mechanisms to distribute student financial aid helped secure the primacy of market forces in the shaping of American higher education.
>
> (Zemsky et al., 2005: 177)

There seems to be general agreement that increased cost sharing should be accompanied by adequate levels of support for student living expenses, and that this in turn justifies some degree of subsidy, from the state or from individual institutions. Several writers (e.g., Ward and Douglass, 2006: 6) refer to this as a "moderate fee/high aid" regime. Such subsidies comprise scholarships and other grants to households; student loans and scholarships; and other grants to households attributable for educational institutions, but with increasing recourse to loans (institutional aid) (Vincent-Lancrin, 2009: 142). One major issue for those designing and implementing subsidy schemes is how to ensure that the subsidies, and in particular non-repayable aid (which includes loan remissions, tax credits and fee reductions as well as grants), are put to the best use in facilitating access.

It seems clear that finance (not only fees but also living costs while studying) is only one of the barriers to more equitable participation in higher education. But it is a barrier for some students from low income backgrounds, even those who are able to overcome the academic barriers that many of them face. The evidence suggests that for these students, non-repayable aid, in the form of upfront grants, is the best approach:

> It is not because they are short of money at the time they go to post-secondary education; if that were the problem, then loans would likely suffice since debt aversion does not seem to be a problem. Rather, it is because lower-income youth evaluates the cost-benefit ratio of post-secondary education [PSE] in a systematically different way from wealthier youth. This makes them less likely to see post-secondary education in a positive light and therefore more in need of financial inducement to "tip the balance" of the decision in favour of enrolling and remaining in PSE.
>
> (Usher, 2006: 24; cf. Heller, 2006: 21 and 2007: 44)

But whilst some national systems target grants and other forms of non-repayable aid on such students (e.g., Australia, New Zealand, the UK, which have also moved away from subsidizing tuition), others (e.g., the US, some parts of Canada) have moved in the opposite direction, either spreading subsidy widely through tax credits that mainly benefit the middle classes or, at State or institutional level, supplementing need-based aid with merit-based aid that is effectively class-blind and does nothing to improve participation because it mostly goes to students who would have entered higher education anyway given their family backgrounds. We shall look at equity in a moment but first there is one other issue regarding student aid, namely the relationship between the means of funding teaching and the means of funding aid.

As has already been noted, in the US the decision was taken in the early 1980s to fund some portion of teaching through Federal aid. In a recent commentary, Alexander criticizes the perverse effects of an uncoordinated Federal/State funding regime:

> For nearly four decades federal government policy has had a somewhat perverse effect on higher education by disproportionately aiding institutions that charge more while at the same time also providing financial incentives to states that opt out of funding of their public colleges and universities.
>
> (Alexander, 2008: 172)

The issue here is not whether Alexander is right but the need for financing regimes for education and aid to march together with common goals and intended impacts (cf., Hauptman, 2001; St John and Priest, 2006; Ehrenberg, 2006).[10]

Equity

It has been argued so far that teaching should be funded through a combination of institutional grants and fees; that as the proportion of institutional funding that is privately sourced increases (to a maximum of 45–50 percent), the state should fund institutions through negotiated development plans that reflect both public and institutional aims and objectives (and should also embrace research and other core activities); and that the best way of reconciling students still at school to their higher educational costs is through a combination of up-front, means tested grants and a graduate tax. There is however one final issue, equity.

In considering funding regimes for education, considerable attention is paid to the issue of equitable access for students. But there is also an equity issue for institutions, and indeed the two are linked since (as we saw in Chapter 3) in a number of countries with marketized or semi-marketized systems, students from lower income and ethnic minority backgrounds tend to attend the less well-resourced universities and colleges. This means that the wealthiest students with the greatest social capital have the most spent on their postsecondary education.

According to the College Board (2007: 25), expenditures on instruction in 2005–06 averaged $16,300 per student at American private doctoral universities, $9,400 at public doctoral universities and $5,000 at public four year undergraduate colleges. One of the main reasons for these differentials was the widely varying levels of endowment. Winston (2000) calculated that institutional savings (a school's accumulation of wealth, physical and financial, with which to support future non-tuition income to pay for future student subsidies and/or educational spending) varied over the previous decade between $8,754 and $1,175 for the top and bottom deciles of private institutions, with a sector average of $2,676, and between $1,335 and $334 for public institutions, with a sector average of $577. These disparities were likely to grow as the wealthy institutions in each sector used their resources to increase their attractiveness to students and donors. It is true that the "credit crunch" will have reduced, at least temporarily, the absolute value of this wealth but, as a recent letter in *The Chronicle* (Munson, 2009) pointed out, their value remains huge, as do the differentials with less well-endowed institutions.

In the UK, Brown and Ramsden (2006) found that, taking together teaching and research income per weighted full-time equivalent (FTE) student and allowing for subject mix, the best funded institution enjoyed an income of up to two and a half times the mean sectoral figure, whilst the least well-funded institution had an income of under half the mean (2004–05 figures). (The index ranged from 247 percent for Imperial College of Science, Technology and Medicine to 40 percent for Edge Hill College, now Edge Hill University.) Even allowing for the by now tediously rehearsed problems with information about quality, there is no obvious way in which resourcing differences of this magnitude can be justified.

It is therefore suggested that, as well as having a mechanism for monitoring the composition of the student body in terms of under-represented groups, there should be a means in each system for controlling differences of this kind, and especially for ensuring a minimum (and possibly also a maximum) level of resourcing per student. This could be done by reviewing institutional resourcing (including the resourcing of research) on a regular basis, and adjusting the funding of those institutions that fulfil a valuable societal role, for example, through their efforts in widening participation or through assisting their local and regional economies, so that they are less heavily disadvantaged. Plan-based funding is the obvious mechanism. Hauptman (2001) suggested that average cost per student across the system in each subject area should be the basis of funding. Bowen et al. (2005) also argue for a more differentiated approach to institutional funding, with public flagships given greater freedom to set tuition and the "regional" universities and many state and community colleges having lower tuition but more generous State and Federal funding.

Besides monitoring institutional resource levels (and efficiency of resource usage), and adjusting levels of institutional subsidy, the funding authority

institutional and departmental levels, and it has to be done by experts, on a regular basis.

Whilst student, employer and government inputs may all be helpful, minimum standards of provision can only be established, for all its weaknesses, through peer review. For this purpose, there needs to be a mechanism through which appropriate peers external to the provision being evaluated periodically evaluate:

- The aims and purposes of the program(s) and the awards concerned;
- Whether those aims and purposes are being achieved, and whether the institution is doing all in its power to enable students to achieve them (by giving them the requisite opportunities and resources);
- Whether those aims and purposes are worthwhile;
- How the department/institution satisfies itself on those matters.

In arriving at their judgments, the assessors will be guided by any generally agreed benchmarks, codes, etc. The UK has an "academic infrastructure", devised by the former Higher Education Quality Council, consisting of a qualifications framework, a code of quality assurance, "benchmark statements" setting out the general aims and purposes of the curriculum in a wide range of subjects, and a template for "program specifications" in all subjects (Brown, 2004: 140). This approach to defining standards is being adopted internationally, for instance through the European Tuning Project: (http://tuning.unideusto.org/tuningeu), whilst Adelman (2008) has recently suggested that it should be adopted in the US. Assessors will need to consider how far students are genuinely engaged in the development and implementation of courses and assessments.[13]

Ideally, in a mature system, this system of curriculum review will be an institutionally owned one, with the assessors' reports being made to the institutional authorities and the efficacy of the process being tested through institutional review. In a still developing system, however, the review panels might be constituted by, and report to, the regulatory agency (see later).

Outcomes

Ultimately the outcomes of any quality assurance process depend on the primary purpose(s). The main issues are whether review reports should be published, whether they should incorporate any grades, and what the consequences should be for the department or institution being assessed. These are of course interrelated.

Publication

It is hard to see how even a limited accountability purpose can be served if the outcomes of external quality assurance are not placed in the public domain, and this is increasingly the trend. The main argument against, which applies to the reports of the regional accrediting commissions in the US, is that publication may lead to a lack of frankness and make the implementation of findings and recommendations harder. This seems a difficult argument to make, especially as other respected external processes, such as institutional audit, have successfully achieved their objectives despite publication (not only of the judgments but also the reasons for those judgments) for many years.

Grading

The issue here is whether to have a purely formative judgment (identifying strengths, weaknesses, issues for further consideration, etc.); a "weak" summative judgment (pass/fail possibly with strengths, weaknesses etc.); or a "strong" summative judgment (grades such as 1 equals outstanding, 2 equals satisfactory, 3 equals unsatisfactory etc.). Although preferable on educational grounds, it must be doubtful whether a purely formative judgment meets basic accountability requirements. On the other hand, grading not only lays those making the judgments open to all sorts of challenges on grounds of fairness, consistency, etc. but can also lead to games playing (on both sides).

Consequences

The issue here is what consequences an external quality assurance process should have for the department or institution being evaluated. It can be argued that in an increasingly competitive world, where reputation is ever more important, even the publication of a critical report can have damaging consequences for the institution or department concerned. In practice, given that there is usually public money involved, there is an argument for at least leaving open the possibility also of a loss of funding, a loss of status (de-accreditation) or even both, in the event that severe weaknesses are discovered and/or minimum standards are being breached (in which case, the department/institution concerned should be given a timescale for producing an action plan to deal with the problem).

Ownership

There are now very few purely self-regulatory systems. In the UK, self-regulation was surrendered by the Vice-Chancellors in 1996 in return for a quite illusory reduction in "bureaucracy" (Brown, 2004). On the other hand, even government-established agencies often involve a considerable degree of autonomy (Santiago et al., 2008: 281). In fact, most systems involve a combination of self-, market- and state- regulation. There are obvious dangers with each. Self-regulation can be too cosy and inward-looking. Government-run agencies may be too susceptible to executive influence. Market-regulation faces the insuperable problem of adequate consumer information (for a recent review, see Dill and Beerkens, 2009). A fourth variant—given the need for the agency to be both accountable and independent of both the institutions and the government—is for the quality agency to be answerable to the legislature. Thus in Britain the Quality Assurance Agency or its successor could report to Parliament, rather like the Comptroller and Auditor General who oversees the use made of public funds. The rationale would be that in view of higher education's key role as the gatekeeper and accreditor of knowledge (and status), especially the knowledge needed for the professions, it needs and deserves special treatment so that it is not dominated by institutions, government or consumers. In an ideal system, the state development agency would be responsible to the government and legislature for the public funding of institutions (and students) whilst the quality agency would report to the legislature on the uses made of those funds for both teaching and research.

Quality Control of the Regulator

Quis custodiet? How to ensure that the regulatory agency itself remains effective? There is already beginning to be some international self-regulation. The International Association of Quality Assurance Agencies in Higher Education (INQAAHE) has issued Guidelines (www. inquaahe.org). In Europe, a Register of quality assurance agencies has been established (Bologna Secretariat, 2007). It is suggested that regulatory agencies should be subject to periodic (every 7–10 years) external review by a team appointed by, and answerable to, the legislature. The team should contain representatives of the main stakeholder interests and an independent chair. Assessors should include the head of another comparable national agency and the head of an agency with cognate responsibilities in another part of the public sector.

An Integrated System

We have talked so far about protecting the quality of student education. However, if research and other forms of scholarly enquiry are evaluated and funded along the lines previously suggested (with only high-cost research evaluated and funded selectively), it makes little sense for the quality of research and the extent to which it meets threshold levels of acceptability to be evaluated separately from teaching. The way would then be clear for a system of departmental review that would look not only at faculty research and student education (incorporating regular peer review of the curriculum being offered) but also at the linkages between them, and indeed the relationships between them and other activities like service, knowledge transfer and community engagement. Departmental review could either be an internal process, the outcomes of which were tested through periodic institutional review or it could, for still developing systems, be an external process organized by the regulatory agency. This takes us neatly to the relationship between research and teaching.[14]

The Relationship between Research and Teaching

As we noted in Chapter 3, one of the major impacts of marketization has been to fragment academic activities or, at least, to reinforce the fragmentation that is already being driven by the huge expansion and specialization of knowledge (Calhoun, 2006). One important area where this has occurred has been in the relationship between research and teaching, especially through the increased selectivity of research funding (Clark, 1991) and the increased commercialization of research (Rinne and Koivula, 2005; White, 2007). Another major factor is the greater esteem accorded to research in many institutions (Boyer Commission, 1998; Court, 1999; White, 2007; Attwood, 2009a), though this may change as institutions become more reliant on teaching revenue (Heppner, 2009).

This separation is damaging, for several reasons:

- As we have seen, it is the conduct of research (including the ability to offer research degrees) which in many countries distinguishes universities from non-university institutions. If less research is conducted, or if research is concentrated into fewer institutions, that distinction weakens or disappears, together with the justification for the additional costs. It also reduces the attractiveness of an academic career for many faculties;
- As we have also seen, it is performance in research which underpins institutional hierarchies in many systems (as well as the international league tables). There is an important value for money issue if research does not benefit teaching in those (and other) institutions, especially as teaching income is often used to cross-subsidize research, either directly or through lower teaching loads for active researchers;
- A major societal benefit of higher education is the embodiment of new knowledge and new technologies in human capital which in turn contributes to economic and social development as graduates—and not only graduates in science and technology—enter the workforce (McMahon, 2009: 94). This embodiment cannot happen if the creation of new knowledge and technologies is divorced from their dissemination;
- If the link is broken, the justification for funding research in universities (as opposed to research institutes) is weaker. Logically indeed there is no reason to conduct research in universities *unless* it benefits student learning. Breaking the link would make universities (in countries where research and teaching are conducted side by side) more dependent on other, and fewer, sources of funding (Johnstone and Marcucci, 2007:

or articulate clearly with other forms of postsecondary education. A state-controlled development agency should channel public funds to universities and colleges and, together with the regulatory agency, ensure that the institutions collectively deliver a range of public and private goods in accordance with the declared purposes of the system;

– Academic research and inquiry should be funded on a dual basis. In areas where research is disproportionately costly to conduct it should be funded on a competitive and selective basis using peer review and performance indicators such as citations and external income. The state, through the regulatory agency, should monitor and control the degree of concentration that results. All other research and inquiry should be funded pro rata to the staff effort involved, with performance being audited through an integrated process of institutional and departmental review. The regulatory agency should also monitor the implementation and effectiveness of safeguards on commercially funded or sponsored research and educational programs;

– Teaching should be funded through a mixture of institutional grants and tuition fees with the proportion of the latter capped at 45–50 percent. Grants would be based on development plans showing how the institution concerned intended to achieve its mission over the relevant period. Fee competition should be limited (any significant local cost differences would be picked up through the grant mechanism). Overall resourcing differentials between institutions should be controlled by the state, with a guaranteed minimum (and possible maximum) of public funding for each student;

– A system of maintenance grants should be available to help students from low-income backgrounds meet their living costs while attending college (institutional needs-based aid could supplement this but variations between institutions would be carefully controlled). Beyond this, income contingent loans would be available to help meet both fees and maintenance, with the loans repayable on an equitable basis, preferably through some form of "graduate tax". There should be policy coordination between the funding of teaching and the funding of maintenance;

– Quality should be monitored by a system-wide regulatory agency accountable to the state legislature. Institutional and departmental review should ensure minimum standards of student learning achievement and academic practice. Both the agency and institutions should be guided by general statements about the characteristics of programs and awards likely to fulfil those standards. Particular attention should be paid in both forms of review to the ways in which institutions ensure that they have a workforce that is fit for purpose. The agency should have the power to recommend the de-accreditation of any institution that consistently fails to meet minimum standards of governance, management or quality;

– Research and teaching should be linked through making the achievement of links a legal requirement for universities and degree-granting institutions; making it a prerequisite for public research funding; auditing the achievement of links through quality review; and targeted initiatives and the identification of good practice.

Together, these policies should over time take any higher education system closer to the desired model. But there are four areas where further comment may be appropriate.

The Role of the Institutions

Universities and colleges are ultimately creatures of society and for the past 20 years or so the policy trend has been toward market competition. But institutions in many systems already enjoy a considerable degree of autonomy, whilst in others their autonomy is increasing. Universities and colleges also have a wider role as critic and conscience of society. As Calhoun (2006) and others have suggested, part of the problem with marketization is that many institutions, administrators and faculty have been complicit in creating or permitting some of the detriments of competition. Within this, the role of the elite institutions and their leaders and spokesmen is crucial since they are the people whom policymakers, the media and the wider public take most notice of. Yet as Eckel (2007: 91) points out: "those best positioned to lead [such] change are the very same institutions that are benefitting the most from the current system of competition" (cf. Breneman, 2008). The same could be said in the UK and Australia.[16]

Representativeness of the Student Population

These policies will make only a limited contribution to this objective. The basic causes of differential participation lie far back in the economic, social and educational systems, and require interventions at those stages (Brown, 2007b). However, we need to avoid exacerbating the problem at the university level by, for example, using assessments that largely reflect socioeconomic status and acquired social capital (for SAT scores, see Bowen 2004b; for A levels, see Gorard et al., 2006). Plan-based funding could be a means of incentivizing institutions to recruit students from backgrounds unfamiliar with higher education, whilst the reduction over time of unjustified resourcing differentials between institutions will help less prestigious institutions to become both more attractive to, and better able to cater for, larger numbers of such students (they would also be assisted by better and clearer progression routes both within the system and without, which a local or regional higher education "system" would facilitate).

Quality of the Academic Workforce

In most systems faculty and other staff are either employed by individual institutions or, even where they are employed by the state, actually deployed by institutions. Actions to determine the quantity and quality of staff are therefore a matter for institutions rather than the state or the system as a whole. Nevertheless, the proposal that the development agency should have a specific remit in relation to staff, together with the inclusion of the recruitment, deployment, management and development of staff as foci of attention in both forms of regulatory review, should signal the importance to the system of having a well-organized, well-equipped and well-motivated workforce if the objectives set for the system are to be achieved (for an outstanding discussion of the issues, see Enders and Musselin, 2007).

Adequacy of Funding

Looking across the OECD countries we see a huge range of expenditures per student. Some of these differentials reflect differences in national wealth but this is only a part of the explanation. It is suggested that the aim should be a level of expenditure that is within some sort of range of the mean for systems of comparable size (i.e., participation and graduation) and wealth (GDP per capita). Similarly, public expenditure on research should bear some relationship to the OECD averages. The aim would be to have an appropriate level or range of expenditure for systems at a comparable stage of development.[17]

A Balanced System

If applied in a considered and integrated manner, the outcome of these policies would be a system that:

- Recognizes, balances and promotes the multiple and distinct public and private purposes of universities and colleges;
- Protects university autonomy but also recognizes the obligations that universities have to the society that gives them that autonomy;
- Recalls universities to their core functions of creating, conserving and disseminating knowledge for its own sake, rather than for the sake of gaining reputation or resources;
- Acknowledges the pressures on public expenditure, and therefore uses that money to control unjustified, and societally dysfunctional, differentials between different institutions and categories of students;
- Makes the best use of necessarily limited information about quality;
- Introduces or maintains competition for students and research funds within an overall division of institutional labor;

- Ensures at least minimum standards of quality for both student education and faculty research;
- Links student education and faculty research, and therefore offers students, research funders and society as a whole the best value for their commitment to, and investment in, higher education.

In short, a balanced higher education system.

Notes

1. Martinez and Richardson (2003: 897) also use the phrase "a balanced system" but describe one where the interests of the institutions, the state and the market are in broad equilibrium, whereas what is meant here is a system where there is a balance between public and private objectives and interests.
2. Douglass and Keeling (2008: 6–7) point out that, at the graduate level, the American public universities tend to offer a greater variety of professional programs to meet societal needs, such as nursing, veterinary medicine and optometry; private institutions tend to have fewer academic degree programs and are wary of high cost and perceived low-prestige professional fields and programs.
3. The 2001 RAE had a median effect on total university revenue of less than 1 percent, with an institutional maximum of 3.7 percent (Sastry and Bekhradnia, 2006). In Australia, the Composite Index covered only 7 percent of institutions' research funding. The US National Research Council rankings (in 1983, 1995, and recently, with the results still to be announced) do not involve any money at all.
4. Geuna and Martin (2003: 303) contrast a performance-based system with one based on educational size, the benefits and costs of which are the reverse of those of a performance-based one. They recommend a "hybrid" system based partly on performance (incentive creating) and partly on educational size (cost minimizing). McMahon (2009: 270) proposes that at institutional level the cost of producing an article/book (and possibly a PhD) should be the basis for directing research investment.
5. One of the most celebrated cases concerned the agreement between the Novartis Company and the Department of Plant and Microbial Biology at the University of California, Berkeley, whereby the Company paid over $25m over 5 years in return for the right to review in advance all proposed publications based on research supported by it (or by the Federal government) and to ask the University to apply for a patent on any findings contained in the research (Bok, 2003: 151–53). Even more worrying are the secret agreements between the University of Pennsylvania and Pfizer and IBM about university research sponsored by them and described in Greenberg (2007: 270–74).
6. Douglass and Keeling (2008: 17) mention as issues to be addressed in this context:

   - Robust financial aid programs that are adequately funded at a level that reduces the net cost to targeted populations;
   - Gradual increases of tuition and fee prices in relation to a schedule of long-term financing of public higher education;

- Student choice—particularly at the undergraduate level, differential pricing may skew student choices, creating market forces that would be heavily influenced by a student's economic background;
- Financial aid and inter-institutional revenue sharing. Within state public systems (US) and national systems (UK), a natural question is how might new fee-generated revenue work into a general scheme of revenue sharing specifically for financial aid;
- Campus revenue sharing, or will the rich get richer? Public universities have only recently adopted differential fees. They are often making choices without clear norms or well-scrutinized goals beyond the search for new revenues. Without a strong commitment to revenue sharing from the outset, increasingly powerful academic units will resist allocations based on shared revenues in their own individual quest for quality and prestige.

The strong resistance of the elite Russell Group universities in the UK to the notion of national bursaries (institutional aid grants set at a common level) bears out the last point. Douglass and Keeling also show how increasingly the fees/prices charged by the leading institutions in both the US and Europe are influenced by international competition.

7. Douglass and Keeling (2008: 15) refer to a 1973 Carnegie Commission report which proposed, on the basis of an estimate of the proportionate public and private benefits, a threefold division of costs: students and their families; State government; and institutional sources, including Federal financial support. Johnstone and Marcucci (2007: 18) estimate that in-State four-year public sector tuition fees in the US are generally in the range of 30–40 or 45 percent of actual costs, before the offsetting sums in financial assistance are factored in. As already noted, McMahon (2009: 30) estimates that the wider social benefits of higher education, including research, represent 52 percent of the total benefits.

8. Before we leave this issue, Mongolia appears to be the only country where there is no state subsidy of any kind for student education (Johnstone and Marcucci, 2007: 20).

9. Newman and Couturier (2002: 11) proposed the idea of "charter universities" whereby the state negotiates a budget with the university but the institution can qualify for "bonus funding" based on performance in such areas as measurement of learner outcomes (sic); partnerships with elementary and secondary schools; diversity of enrollments by socioeconomic status, race and ethnicity; and service to the community. Massy (2004: 31) proposed "performance-based steering", where a small amount of funding is based on the evaluation of key elements of performance by the funding authority, with the evaluation made public. Such a mechanism "nudges universities in directions judged to be in the public interest, but it does not overpower them". Newman et al. (2004: 128–29) suggested that State-wide "compacts" should include, to meet State needs: academic success for an ever expanding share of the population, efficient use of university resources, academic recognition that teaching and learning matter, preserving the integrity of scholarship, preparing students for tomorrow's democracy, and deepening outreach and service.

Salmi and Hauptman (2006: 9) distinguished performance contracts, performance set-aside, competitive funds and payment for results (ibid.: 10); some of
these can be combined with non-performance related mechanisms. The advantages include greater transparency (if the performance measures are publicly
developed and readily available); a better linkage to public policy objectives (as
opposed to institutional needs); and greater accountability. However, such methods tend to be more inflexible in their operation, can lead to greater year to year
variation in funding if performance results vary (and thus contribute to instabil-
ity), and may discourage both diversity and autonomy (ibid.: 44).

A number of US States have experimented with various forms of performance-
related funding, typically allocating a small proportion of funds against agreed
measures. The literature surveyed (Zumeta, 2001; Martinez and Nilson, 2006;
Aldeman and Carey, 2008; Lederman, 2008; Dougherty and Natow, 2009) suggests that the results have been mixed in terms of efficiency, effectiveness and
access. The key success determinants appear to include: (1) the proportion of
funds involved (which needs to be large enough to be taken seriously by institutions); (2) the funding climate (whether overall funding is improving and whether
"new" money is available to ease the transition); (3) the availability of information; (4) the extent to which institutions are involved in designing the process; (5)
the amount of public/legislator interest. In their study of performance funding in
South Dakota between 1997 and 2002, Martinez and Nilson also point to the
importance of one public entity (in this case, the Board of Regents covering all the
State's universities) taking responsibility for affordability and the fees charged.

Studies of European performance-based systems (Holtta and Rekila, 2003;
Gornitzka et al., 2004; Schenker-Wicki and Hurlimann, 2006; Treuthardt and
Valimaa, 2008) are also equivocal. However, the context is rather different
because there the state is trying to give the institutions greater autonomy, and
strengthen institutional leadership rather than, as in the US, secure greater
responsiveness to public interests. The most specific of the studies—Schenker-
Wicki and Hurlimann's study of the performance contracts introduced in
Switzerland in the 1990s—suggests that in the absence of complementary changes
within the institutions, significant efficiency improvements had yet to occur
(2006: 63–65).

By contrast, the kind of performance funding advocated here—plan-based
funding—would be within a context of autonomous institutions with well-
developed managerial and analytical capabilities; would entail a considerable
amount of negotiation; would be introduced gradually; would eventually cover all
of an institution's public funding; would take account of both institutional and
sector-wide performance indicators; would involve annual monitoring between
settlements; and would produce outcomes controlled for quality and expenditure
per student. It therefore represents a feasible means of reconciling the needs of
individual universities and colleges with the objectives of public policy, especially
responsiveness, institutional diversity and service to society (Kezar, 2005). In this
context it may be worth quoting van Vught's recent remarks about Hong Kong:

> The [University Grants Committee] entered into an open discussion with
> each of the (eight) universities of the Hong Kong higher education system

and stimulated them to formulate their specific missions and roles in the context of the broader system. Subseqently, these missions and roles were formalised in agreements between the individual institutions and the UGC. During this process the UGC kept its eye on its objective to increase the diversity at the level of the system. Finally, after a few years, the UGC developed a "Performance and Role-related Funding Scheme", in which it explored, together with the individual institutions, whether they had been able to remain within the parameters of their mission and role statements. The result was a clear increase of the diversity of the Hong Kong higher education system and even a growing enthusiasm with the institutions to stick to their roles (van Vught, 2008: 165–66).

10. One other issue concerning aid is the need for the relevant administrative processes to be as straightforward as possible consistent with accountability. Referring to Pell Grants, Bowen et al. (2005: 203) say that the problem is not so much the reduction over time in real value as the complexity of the application process and the obscure connection between family characteristics and aid. The new US administration has the simplification of Federal student aid as one of its key higher education objectives (Baum and McPherson, 2009)

11. Winston (1999: 31–32) describes how in the early 1990s the Department of Justice banned the coordination of tuition and financial aid between leading private institutions. Kirp and Holman (2003: 31–32) propose a series of "arms control agreements" between institutions covering things like expenditure on "frills" and need-based aid. However market forces are almost certainly now too strong for such voluntary action. Kirp appears to accept this: "with the prize to the winner and the price borne by the losers so great, only rarely is a school willing to take the lead" (2003b: 263; for a similar conclusion, see Ehrenberg, 2002: 78).

12. Volkwein and Grunig (2005) contrast three separate models of educational excellence: resources and reputation (favored by the academy), strategic investment (the civic and governmental community) and client-centered (parents, students and student affairs professionals) (cf. Westerheijden, 2007: 78; Sweitzer and Volkwein, 2009).

13. At the Copenhagen Business School students are involved in every level of academic decision making, with 50 percent membership of the "study committees" that develop and maintain programs. This leads to a significant student role in shaping and renewing programs, without usurping the roles and prerogatives of faculty (Riddersholm and Kjersner, 2002). The author is indebted to Lee Harvey for this reference. According to a recent survey by the UK National Union of Students, only 23 percent of students feel involved in shaping the content, curriculum or design of their courses yet 57 percent would welcome such involvement (National Union of Students, 2009: 3).

14. Before leaving the regulator, we should note three other system-wide functions that are complementary to those already outlined:

   – Responding to complaints about quality of provision, including academic standards, that have not been resolved for this purpose (the UK has a special regulator for this purpose);

- Validating institutions' claims about quality in things like prospectuses, websites, marketing material etc. This is done to a limited extent in UK institutional audit. This could be done through regular reviews but might also be handled through response to complaints;
- Producing an annual report on quality developments in the system, including the identification of any factors that may have affected attempts to maintain or improve quality.

15. The FHEQ Descriptor for a Bachelor's degree with honors requires, inter alia, that a student demonstrates "a systematic understanding of key aspects of their field of study, including acquisition of coherent and detailed knowledge, at least some of which is at, or informed by, the forefront of defined aspects of a discipline" http://www.qaa.ac.uk/academicinfrastructure/FHEQ/EWNI08/FHEQ08.pdf [accessed on July 24, 2009]. The PSF includes the ability to "incorporate research, scholarship and/or professional practice" into student learning in each of the three Standards that lecturers and appropriate support staff have to meet whilst the "Integration of scholarship, research and professional activities with teaching and supporting learning" is one of the six areas of activity to which the Standards apply. http://www.heacademy.ac.uk/assets/York/documents/ourwork/ProfesssionalStandardsFramework.pdf [accessed on July 24, 2009]

16. In this context, one other irony that may be worth remarking upon is the fact that so much of the American literature that is critical of many aspects of marketization comes from scholars who have either been leaders of distinguished institutions or have worked there. The former include men like Bok (twice President of Harvard), William Bowen (Princeton), Duderstadt (Michigan State) and Ehrenberg (Cornell). The latter include Dill (University of North Carolina, Chapel Hill), Douglass (University of California, Berkeley), Massy (Stanford), Winston (Williams College) and Zemsky (University of Pennsylvania).

17. According to *Education at a Glance 2008* (OECD, 2008), annual expenditure on educational core services per student in 2005 in US dollars at Purchasing Power Parity rates for the OECD countries where there was data ranged from $4,273 in the Slovak Republic to $18,656 in the US; the mean average was $7,976. For research the range was $652 (Slovak Republic) to $8,694 (Switzerland), the average being $3,391. Expenditure per student including advanced research programs as a percentage of per capita GDP at Purchasing Power Parity ranged from 29 (Italy) to 65 (Switzerland). The latter, which measures propensity to spend on higher education institutions, is arguably a better measure of national commitments to higher education.

Notes on Contributors

Alberto Amaral is President of Portuguese higher education's Evaluation and Accreditation Agency. He was Director of CIPES and has been chair of the Board of CHER. He is life member of IAUP and a member of EAIR, SHRE, SCUP and IMHE. He is editor and co-editor of several books, including *Governing Higher Education: National Perspectives on Institutional Governance*, *The Higher Education Managerial Revolution? Markets in Higher Education: Rhetoric or Reality?* and *Reform and Change in Higher Education.*

Paulo Charles Pimentel Bótas is a Research Officer/Lecturer at ICHEM—School of Management, University of Bath. He holds a PhD in Sociology/Policy Studies from the Institute of Education, University of London. He has carried out research on students' perceptions of quality teaching in higher education in the UK, the academic labor market in the UK, and an evaluation of the tools for assessing the quality of students' experience and engagement in higher education—NSS, CEQ, NSSE and AUSSE. Currently, he is researching governance, diversity, labor market and the Bologna process, and modernization of higher education. He has published articles in the *Higher Education Review* and *Educate*. His interests are: quality assurance, teaching and learning, new managerialism, marketization, critical and feminist pedagogies, cognitive psychology and psycho-analytical perspectives of teaching and learning, social and cultural capital, and power relations in higher education.

Roger Brown is Professor of Higher Education Policy and Co-Director of the Centre for Research and Development in Higher Education at Liverpool Hope University. He was previously Vice Chancellor of Southampton Solent University, Chief Executive of the Higher Education Quality Council, Chief Executive of the Committee of Directors of Polytechnics and Secretary of the Polytechnics and Colleges Funding Council. He has served on many national committees and boards. He has written a book *Quality Assurance in Higher Education: The UK Experience since 1992* (2004) and many articles and lectures on different aspects of HE policy. He is currently a Visiting Professor or equivalent at London Metropolitan University, Edinburgh Napier University, the University of Southampton and the Open University. He was elected a Vice President of the Society for Research in Higher Education in 2007.

Lydia Hartwig is Managing Director and Deputy Head of the Bavarian State Institute for Higher Education Research and Planning in Munich, Germany.

Before, she worked as a consultant for the German Council of Science and Humanities, the advisory body to the Federal Government and State Governments in Germany. She holds a PhD in German Literature. Lydia Hartwig has worked on various issues of higher education, especially financing, governance and management of higher education institutions, quality assurance and academic careers. She is also editor of the journal "Beiträge zur Hochschulforschung".

Seppo Hölttä is Professor of Higher Education Administration and Finance at the Department of Management Studies, University of Tampere, Finland. He is the head of both, the Higher Education Group and the Finnish Graduate School for Higher Education Administration, Management and Economics. During his career he has worked both in academic and administrative positions in several Finnish universities. He has international experience as a Fulbright scholar at the University of California and a visiting professor at Michigan State University. His research interests include the internal dynamics and functions of universities, and theoretical and empirical research on higher education systems and policies. He has published widely in journals such as *Higher Education Policy, European Journal of Education* and written several book chapters.

Futao Huang is Professor of the Research Institute for Higher Education, Hiroshima University, Japan. He finished his doctoral courses in both China and Japan. His major interests include: (1) a comparative study of university curricular development; (2) policy changes, organizations, structures and governance patterns relating to higher education in the comparative perspectives with a focus on China and Japan; (3) internationalization of higher education in East Asia. Since the 1990s, he has published widely in Chinese, English and Japanese languages in many international peer-reviewed journals, including *Higher Education, Higher Education Policy, Policy and Management of Higher Education, Journal of Studies in International Education* and other Chinese and Japanese journals. Currently, he is also Guest Professor of Peking University, Shanghai Jiaotong University and other Chinese universities.

Tea Jansson is Planning Officer in the Higher Education Group at the Department of Management Studies, University of Tampere, Finland. She works as the Administrator of the international joint degree Master program, European Master in Higher Education, which has been awarded the status of Erasmus Mundus program by the European Commission and the Finnish Graduate School for Higher Education Administration, Management and Economics. She holds an MA in English Philology and Women Studies from the University of Tampere. Currently she is finalizing her Master of Science degree in Administrative Science, especially in the field of Higher Education Administration. Her research interests include gender issues, internationalization

—— (Ed.) (2002) *The Future of the City of Intellect.* Stanford: University Press.

Brown, N. (2001) *Funding by Mission: An Exploration of the Public Funding of Higher Education Institutions on the Basis of Business Plans.* London: Standing Conference of Principals (now Guild HE).

Brown, N. & Ramsden, B. (2006) *Measuring the Prosperity of UK Higher Education Institutions.* (Unpublished research commissioned by the author).

Brown, R. (2004) *Quality Assurance in Higher Education: The UK Experience since 1992.* London: RoutledgeFalmer.

—— (2006). League tables—do we have to live with them? *Perspectives,* 10(2): 33–38.

—— (2007a). *The Information Fallacy.* Higher Education Policy Institute. http://www.hepi.ac.uk/pubdetail.asp?ID = 229&DOC = Seminars [Accessed on August 06, 2009].

—— (2007b) Reeking hypocrisy? New Labour and widening participation in higher education. *Perspectives,* 11(4): 97–102.

—— (2008) How do we get more effective policies for higher education? Reflections of a policymaker. *Higher Education Review,* 41(1): 3–20.

—— (2009a) "Where the US goes today . . ." Oxford: Higher Education Policy Institute. http://www.hepi.ac.uk/pubdetail.asp?ID = 279&DOC = 3 [Accessed on August 09, 2009].

—— (2009b) The changing architecture of quality assurance. Paper presented to *The Australian Universities Quality Forum,* Alice Springs. http://www.auqa.edu.au/files/auqf/paper/brown [Accessed on July 01, 2009].

Burke, J. C. (2005) The Many Faces of Accountability. In Burke, J. & Associates (Eds) *Achieving Accountability in Higher Education: Balancing Public, Academic and Market Demands.* San Francisco: Jossey-Bass.

Byrne, R. (2008) The gap persists between faculty salaries at public and private institutions. *The Chronicle of Higher Education* (April 18): np.

Calhoun, C. (2006) The university and the public good. *Thesis Eleven,* 84 (February): 7–43.

Callan, P. M. (2001) Reframing access and opportunity: problematic state and federal higher education policy in the 1990s. In Heller, D. E. (Ed.) *The States and Public Higher Education Policy: Affordability, Access and Accountability.* Baltimore and London: The Johns Hopkins University Press.

Callender, C. (2008) The impact of term-time employment on higher education students' academic attainment and achievement. *Journal of Education Policy,* 23(4): 359–77.

—— (2009) Institutional aid in England: promoting widening participation or perpetuating inequalities? In Knight, J. (Ed.) *Financing Equity and Access in Higher Education.* Rotterdam: Sense Publishing.

Cantor, N. & Levine, S. D. (2006) Taking public scholarship seriously. *The Chronicle of Higher Education* (June 9): np.

Clark, B. R. (1983) *The Higher Education System.* Berkeley and Los Angeles: University of California Press.

—— (1991) The fragmentation of research, teaching and study: an exploratory study. In Trow, M. & Nybom, T. (Eds) *University and Society: Essays on the Social Role of Research and Higher Education.* London: Jessica Kingsley.

Clarke, M. (2005) Quality assessment lessons from Australia and New Zealand. *Higher Education in Europe*, 30 (2): 183–97.

Coaldrake, P. (2000) Rethinking academic and university work. *Higher Education Management*, 12(3): 7–30.

Codling, A. & Van Meek, L. (2006) Twelve propositions on diversity in higher education. *Higher Education Management and Policy*, 18(3): 1–24.

Cohn, E., Rhine, S. L. W. & Santos, M. C. (1989) Institutions of higher education as multi-product firms: economies of scale and scope. *The Review of Economics and Statistics*, 71: 284–90.

Colbeck, C. & Michael, P. W. (2006) The public scholarship: reintegrating Boyer's four domains. *New Directions for Institutional Research*, 129: 7–19.

College Board. (2007) *Trends in College Pricing*. Washington DC: College Board.

Collins, R. (2002) Credential inflation and the future of universities. In Brint, S. (Ed.) *The Future of the City of Intellect*. Stanford: Stanford University Press.

Committee on Higher Education. (1963) *Higher Education*. London: Her Majesty's Stationery Office.

Court, S. (1999) Negotiating the research imperative: the views of UK academics on their career opportunities. *Higher Education Quarterly*, 53(1): 65–87.

Cremonini, L., Westerheijden, D. & Enders, J. (2008) Disseminating the right information to the right audience: cultural determinants in the use (and misuse) of rankings. *Higher Education*, 55(3): 373–85.

D'Andrea, V. & Gosling, D. (2005) *Improving Teaching and Learning in Higher Education: A Whole Institution Approach*. Buckingham: Society for Research in Higher Education and Open University Press.

Dearlove, J. (1997) The academic labour process: from collegiality and professionalism to managerialism and proletarianisation. *Higher Education Review*, 30(1): 56–75.

Deem, R. (1998) "New managerialism" and higher education: the management of performances and cultures in universities in the United Kingdom. *International Studies in Sociology of Education*, 8(1): 47–70.

Deem, R. & Brehony, K. J. (2005) Management as ideology: the case of "new managerialism" in higher education. *Oxford Review of Education*, 31(2): 217–35.

Deem, R., Hillyard, S. & Reed, M. (2007) *Knowledge, Higher Education, and the New Managerialism: The Changing Management of UK Universities*. Oxford: University Press.

Dill, D. & Beerkens, M. (2009) Defining the framework conditions for assuring academic standards: lessons learned about professional, market and government regulation. Paper presented at *The Consortium of Higher Education Researchers (CHER)* 22nd Annual Research Conference on September 11.

Dill, D. D. (2003) Allowing the market to rule: the case of the United States. *Higher Education Quarterly*, 57(2): 136–57.

—— (2007) Will market competition assure academic quality? An analysis of the UK and US experience. In Westerheijden, D. F., Sternsaker, B. & Rosa, M. J. (Eds) *Quality Assurance in Higher Education: Trends in Regulation, Translation and Transformation*. Dordrecht: Springer.

Dill, D. D. & Soo, M. (2005) Academic quality, league tables and public policy: a cross-national analysis of university ranking systems. *Higher Education*, 49(4): 495–533.